MED

MANIFESTATION

SECRETS

THINK, FEEL, AND GROW WEALTHY

E.J HOWARD

PUBLISHED BY GATE7 INTELLECTUAL PROPERTIES

Disclaimer

Neither the publisher nor the author is engaged in rendering legal or any other professional service through this book. If expert assistance is required, the services of appropriate professionals should be sought. The publisher and the author shall have neither liability nor responsibility to any person or entity concerning any loss or damage caused directly or indirectly to the reader by using the information in this book.

Contents

The Concept of Manifestation

Have you ever wanted something so bad you couldn't stop thinking about it? You just had to have it sooner than later? Maybe it's wealth and financial independence, or maybe you are a hopeless romantic, and you want real love in your life. Whatever it is you truly desire, you can acquire. Well, within reason, I mean, you're not going to sprout wings and learn to fly like a bird or bring back the dead or anything like that, but by learning how to correctly apply your God-given gifts of Meditation Manifestation and Affirmations, you will be able to channel your inner powers to call, claim, bring about and manifest your heart's greatest desires.

Ask anyone that believes in the power of **manifesting your 'best life'**; I'm sure they'll entertain you with raving reviews of success stories they have personally experienced.

But even though this way of thinking or, shall I say, process stems from spiritual roots. However, we are going to take a more scientific approach and focus on the aspects that have been proven to work.

So, if you are ready to give affirmations and manifestation a try, then climb aboard, and let's go on a journey of discovery together.

In the following paragraph, we will discuss how Manifestation refers to the ability of a person to change an intangible intention into an external reality. The term was first coined by William James, who also made the distinction between 'willing' and 'vibrating.'

Then we'll discuss what manifestation is, how it can be achieved (both during meditation and externally), and how that works. We will look into the scientific concepts that back manifestation as a viable means of personal power.

We will define what personified manifestation power means and a human being's God-given ability to consciously, as well as subconsciously, transmit their own intentions into an external reality.

Arguably the two most important components of manifestation power are intention and will. When one is fully aware of the world around them at all times, they are able to clearly focus their consciousness on something that they want. If a person intends to manifest something, they are using the power of their will to direct the consciousness that is focused on that intention.

The physical world is directed by the consciousness of humanity. All of the actions and decisions of people, be they individual or collective, have a profound impact on our environment and physical world. This includes both conscious decisions to shape the environment, such as building cities or dams, and unintended consequences, such as pollution or climate change. By understanding our collective responsibility to steward the planet, we can begin to make choices that will manifest a healthier and more sustainable future for all.

It may appear that this concept contradicts many commonly-held conceptions about reality. For example, when one focuses on an intention within their own mind, and nothing happens, it may seem at first that there is no such thing as manifestation. However, those conceptions are based on the limited understanding of reality posited by modern science. The definition of manifestation power given above is based on the philosophy of Vedanta.

Vedanta is the ancient Indian philosophy that reality is

fundamentally consciousness or spirit. This means that everything in the physical world is an externalization of consciousness, including human beings.

Another important component of manifestation power is universal will. Universal will refer to the totality of all manifestations in the universe as a whole. It can be considered a more concrete manifestation of what is commonly termed 'the divine.' It can also be defined as 'the manifested expressions and experiences through which spirit has made itself known.' This means that universal will include all human manifestations, as well as all other manifestations in nature.

The human mind is capable of other states of consciousness that are not easily explained using modern science. It is possible to go into a meditative state, where one's sense of the world becomes very focused and still, and awareness is transferred to a higher level. A person can also enter a 'flow state,' which is a heightened state of consciousness that makes the person feel as if they have achieved success when they are in the flow. The flow state is similar to meditation, but it requires being fully focused on an intention for an extended amount of time. Thus, it produces different effects from meditation. **This means that meditation is a skill that can be used to achieve the flow state and therefore**

manifest an intention.

The above views are not just the opinions of some religious figures but whole traditions which were set up with the aim of making living beings into gods through prayer and/or will alone. This shows that some religion has been meant to keep people in a state where they depend on others rather than themselves for spiritual evolution. Besides the basic understanding of religion as being a study of God's laws and worship, religion has also been created in order to give people an external source of guidance, which can easily be manipulated by a popular minority with power. This is why the concept of spirituality and your true power of self-manifestation have been hidden from the masses.

This secret knowledge was once commonly known to spiritual teachers and sages who taught openly. These teachings were corrupted by false religions that claimed that there were 'gods' who were responsible for everything. They also claimed to be in contact with such 'false gods' and their prophets, which gave them great power and riches over the masses. In time, these claims became so distorted that they caused much separation, suffering, and death to those who believed in them and those who did not.

What Is Meditation Manifestation?

Meditation Manifestation is the belief that directing your focus towards something can bring it into reality. The underlying concept is that the universe responds to your desires and grants them to you. Those who practice manifestation believe that through activities such as journaling, meditation, concentration, or affirmations, they can bring about the manifestation of their desires. According to Jennifer McVey, a Spiritual Life Coach, we are all already manifesting things in our lives. Everything we have and see has already been manifested by us. Becoming aware of our power as creators reminds us that this is a natural process we engage in. Manifestation can involve material things like acquiring a pet or money, as well as more abstract desires such as finding true love.

Manifestation is the foundation of the book *"The Secret,"* which posits that positive thoughts can attract positive events, while negative thoughts can lead to negative outcomes. Suppose you desire to manifest money. In that case, you might engage in practices like visualizing the money in your bank account or meditating on your strong desire to receive a financial windfall.

It's important to note that visualization and meditation alone will not magically bring money to your doorstep the next day. However, if the act of meditation brings you a sense of inner peace and clarity to pursue the career or opportunities that can lead to financial abundance, and if visualization helps you stay focused on your goals, then manifestation has played a role in your progress.

Is Meditation Manifestation Really Real?

If you hold beliefs in a higher power, your religious convictions support it, or you simply have a strong belief in the validity of the laws of attraction, then there is no definitive reason to dismiss its potential truth for you.

On the other hand, according to Spiritual Life Coach Jennifer McVey, if you're new to the concept of manifestation, unaware of its principles, or skeptical about its existence, it might be beneficial to start by focusing on setting and achieving specific goals. Manifestation, after all, revolves around attaining the things you desire.

Does Manifestation Do Anything to You Mentally?

Your mental and emotional well-being can potentially be enhanced through manifestation, leading to an improvement in your overall health.

The most commonly used techniques in manifestation include visualization, journaling, meditation, and positive affirmations. These practices have remarkable benefits for your mental and emotional well-being. They can help reduce stress, uplift your mood, and increase your chances of achieving your goals.

However, it's important to note that if you struggle with anxiety disorders, depression, or obsessive-compulsive disorder, manifestation may not be suitable for you. It's essential to prioritize your mental health and consult with a healthcare professional.

Manifestation requires you to focus on your genuine desires. As suggested by Spiritual Life Coach Jennifer McVey, consider them as "gifts" you want to receive or even give, encompassing emotional, mental, physical, and spiritual aspects. Engaging in this exercise of getting specific about your desires can be enlightening. You may stumble upon something you didn't even realize you wanted initially.

For instance, if you begin manifesting a new car, you might eventually realize that what you truly desire is the freedom that comes with it rather than the vehicle itself. This realization can be incredibly valuable if you believe in the power of subconscious thoughts.

Manifestation can enhance your attitude and keep you focused.

Focusing on your most desired outcome can enhance your capacity to pursue your goals. Moreover, maintaining a positive mindset can greatly influence your overall perspective. To cultivate a more positive attitude towards the pursuit of your goal, visualizing its manifestation can be remarkably beneficial.

Engaging in the practice of manifestation empowers you to feel a sense of control over your own destiny. For individuals inclined towards pessimism, manifestation can serve as a catalyst for transforming your mindset.

Nine Biggest Manifestation Myths Blocking Your Desires

The practice of manifestation and the concept of the law of attraction are gradually gaining global recognition. As a result, an increasing amount of content is being created to elucidate this practice, leading many individuals to question what is genuine and what is spurious. Drawing upon my 25 years of studying and teaching the art of manifestation, I have compiled a list of prevalent manifestation myths and beliefs that I frequently encounter.

Although these statements are indeed myths, they can also be considered limiting beliefs that hinder your ability to manifest your desires. Therefore, it is important to read them attentively and liberate yourself from their influence once and for all. By doing so, you can open yourself up to the full potential of manifestation and unlock the ability to manifest what you truly desire.

Manifestation Myth #1

I just have to think positive thoughts in order to manifest what I want,

It is true that manifestation is not solely about maintaining positive thoughts or visualizing desired outcomes, expecting them to magically materialize. That perspective represents only a fragment of the whole process.

To genuinely manifest what you desire, you must engage in a comprehensive approach that involves thinking, feeling, speaking, acting, believing, and knowing that your desired reality is already an intrinsic part of your identity. Manifestation goes beyond merely manifesting external objects or circumstances; it is about manifesting the essence of who you believe yourself to be. Confidence in what you are manifesting is crucial.

Reflect upon the mindset of a person who already possesses their dream house. How would they think, feel, speak, act, believe, and have an unwavering knowledge of their reality? By consciously embodying these qualities and aligning your current actions and behaviors with that ideal, you can begin to embody the identity of the person who has already achieved their desired outcome.

By focusing on becoming that person in the present, you create a powerful alignment between your beliefs, actions, and aspirations, setting the stage for the manifestation of your dreams.

Manifestation Myth #2

There is no scientific evidence for Manifestation.

Manifestation is often associated with a spiritual practice that is viewed skeptically due to the lack of scientific evidence supporting its claims. However, upon conducting thorough research, one can discover that there is indeed scientific evidence that elucidates the validity of manifestation.

If you wish to dispel your skepticism and embrace the power of your mind, I recommend exploring the following topics on your own:

- Quantum Physics Double Slit Experiment: This experiment in quantum mechanics reveals the role of the observer in influencing the behavior of particles, suggesting that consciousness plays a significant role in shaping reality.

- The Placebo Effect: This phenomenon demonstrates the power of belief and expectation in producing real physiological and psychological effects, even when an inactive substance is administered.

- Dr. Emoto's Water Experiment: The study conducted by Dr. Masaru Emoto explores the influence of thoughts, intentions, and emotions on the molecular structure of water, suggesting that consciousness can affect physical matter.

- Neuroplasticity: Neuroplasticity is the brain's ability to reorganize and form new neural connections in response to experience and mental activity, highlighting the brain's adaptability and its potential for shaping reality.

- Mirror Neurons: Mirror neurons are specialized brain cells that enable us to empathize and imitate the actions, emotions, and intentions of others, emphasizing the interconnectedness between our thoughts, emotions, and the external world.

- Power of Visualization: Research suggests that vivid mental imagery and visualization can enhance motivation, performance, and goal achievement by programming the subconscious mind and influencing actions.

- The Rosenthal Effect: The Rosenthal Effect, also known as the Pygmalion effect, explores how higher expectations placed upon individuals can lead to improved performance and outcomes.

By delving into these subjects, you can gain a deeper understanding of the scientific principles and phenomena that support the concept of manifestation, allowing you to embrace the power of your mind and its potential to shape your reality.

Manifestation Myth #3

You have to do lengthy rituals every day and follow them step by step to make manifestation work for me.

It is indeed a prevalent myth circulating on social media that there is a singular, viral step-by-step manifestation ritual that guarantees results. With the abundance of video content being created daily, there is a tendency to attach excessive structure to the practice, which can create insecurities for beginners. However, it is crucial to recognize that the practice of manifestation is not a one-size-fits-all approach.

It is important to remember that your own intuition should never be ignored simply because someone else suggests a specific way of practicing manifestation. Meditation Manifestation is a fluid process that relies on your intuition, embracing the flow of energy, and taking self-inspired actions that resonate with you personally. YOU have the autonomy to BREAK THE RULES, modify rituals to suit your lifestyle, or even choose not to follow them at all.

Trusting yourself and applying what truly resonates with

you while disregarding what doesn't align is key. Manifestation is a deeply personal journey, and it is vital to honor your own instincts and preferences. Embrace the practices that feel genuine and empowering to you, and let go of any pressure to conform to a rigid set of rules. By cultivating self-trust and authenticity, you can navigate the practice of manifestation in a way that is unique and meaningful to you.

Manifestation Myth #4

Visualizing my desires every day is enough to manifest what I want.

While visualization is a powerful practice in the manifestation process, it is important to understand that it is not the sole factor in manifesting your desires. Many teachers may overlook the significance of taking inspired action, which is an essential part of the process.

Merely visualizing your desired outcomes while remaining inactive is unlikely to bring about the desired results. However, consistent visualization can help align your vibration and energy with what you want to manifest. This alignment can lead to a shift in your perspective, enabling you to recognize and seize opportunities that come your way.

For instance, if your goal is to manifest a car, simply

visualizing it every day without any action is unlikely to magically make the car appear in your garage. However, through consistent visualization, you may become more receptive to intuitive ideas and inspirations. This heightened awareness may lead you to unexpected opportunities, such as deciding to ask for a promotion at work that you previously doubted. By taking inspired action, such as pursuing the promotion, you open up avenues to receive the necessary resources, like a bonus, which can then enable you to purchase the car you desire.

It's essential to remember that visualization serves as a tool to reprogram your subconscious mind, cultivating a belief that your desires are possible for you. However, it is equally important to align your thoughts, feelings, spoken words, beliefs, and identity with your desires. Additionally, being open to taking inspired action when opportunities arise is a crucial step in manifesting your goals.

By combining visualization with aligned thoughts, emotions, beliefs, and inspired actions, you create a powerful synergy that propels you toward manifesting what you truly desire.

Manifestation Myth #5

The Law of Attraction is the only law of the universe.

This is actually not true. Most people are familiar with the law of attraction because it is a popular term used on the internet. They become familiar with it either by watching *The Secret* or hearing it on social media and think that the entire universe operates under this one law. In truth, there are at least 12 main universal laws that all work together to keep our planet in harmony. There may be even more laws we are not currently aware of.

Manifestation Myth #6

I only manifest good things in my life. The unwanted (bad) things are not my fault because I didn't want them. Those are a fluke.

Unfortunately, this statement is just simply not true. According to the principles of the law of attraction, you tend to attract experiences that resonate with your vibrational frequency, regardless of whether they are desirable or not. Even if you don't wish to manifest an undesirable outcome, if your thoughts, emotions, and convictions align with something negative, you inadvertently draw it into your life.

The universal forces operate in a literal and unbiased manner. These laws are indifferent to whether you approve or disapprove of what is being presented to you. Similar to a magnet, you attract what aligns with your vibrational state.

Believing this statement is like suggesting that the law of gravity will solely cause objects of your choosing to fall to the ground while keeping everything else suspended in mid-air.

When you do encounter an undesired experience, it becomes your responsibility to examine any unresolved issues within yourself and identify any subconscious beliefs that might be attracting such experiences into your life.

Manifestation Myth #7

I have to be completely healed and get rid of all my limiting beliefs before I can manifest what I want.

I believe that, as human beings, achieving complete healing or eliminating all limiting beliefs may be an unattainable goal. What adds value to life is our multidimensional nature of existence. Each stage of growth brings forth a new set of limiting beliefs, fresh challenges, and further opportunities for healing throughout our lives.

Therefore, it is indeed possible to embrace the idea of being a work in progress while simultaneously manifesting our desires. You are inherently perfect, with all your imperfections, and deserving of everything you desire in the present moment.

Manifestation Myth #8

It's so much easier to manifest small things than big things.

As much as we want to believe that it's easier to manifest $10 than it is to manifest $1,000,000, it is not. It is actually just as easy to manifest a million then it is a single dollar.

The only reason why it FEELS like it is easier is because we BELIEVE that it is. If we were as sure about a Lamborghini dropping into our garage then we were about a Toyota, we could manifest it just as easily.

The universe doesn't discriminate or know anything about denominations or the monetary value of items you want. It simply gives you what you subconsciously believe is possible for you. That is why letting go of your limiting beliefs and regulating your nervous system when it comes to larger valued items is so important in the manifestation process.

Manifestation Myth #9

Manifestation is a new-age phenomenon, satanic, or related to witchcraft.

Most people think that manifestation and the law of attraction are new-age concepts connected to new-age spirituality (and some even think that the practice of manifestation is connected to satanism or dark witchcraft). However, when you do a little bit of research, you will realize that manifestation is actually found in almost all ancient spiritual texts and is way older than any other religion known to mankind.

New age spirituality has definitely popularized these concepts in recent years and brought them into modern-day life, but manifestation is, in fact, as old as time, similar to how gravity has existed for as long as time.

Saying manifestation is brand new is like saying electricity or gravity is brand new. Just because we only relatively recently learned how to use electricity does not make the laws that make electricity work brand new. They have always existed, just like the laws of the universe that make manifestation work has always existed.

The Difference Between Magic and Manifestation

When I began manifesting the correct way, to others, it seemed like a magic trick.

Manifestation is the process of bringing something into your life through focused thought and deliberate action. It is a form of deliberate creation and is often associated with the law of attraction.

Magic is the use of rituals, symbols, actions, gestures, and language to produce intended results. Magic is often seen as a supernatural force, invoking spirits to do your bidding and always for a price, whereas manifestation is a universal law, seen as a more natural process.

The 12 Universal Laws

We are all familiar with the law of attraction, but did you know that it is just one of the 12 universal laws? Exploring and understanding the other 11 laws can lead us toward a more spiritually aligned life. The concept of the 12 universal laws suggests that there are inherent and unchanging laws governing our universe, which ancient cultures have intuitively understood throughout history. These laws are regarded as highly specific and provide a scientific explanation for the process of manifestation. While some of these laws are associated with Ho'oponopono, a freedom meditation originating in Hawaiian culture, others trace back to the hermetic philosophy of ancient Egypt. These timeless laws continue to be acknowledged and utilized by individuals worldwide, as they all center around mastering life with love and joy, as explained by Kaiser. All of the laws are about mastering our connection with life with love, joy, and happiness.

Let's delve into the essence and significance of each law and explore how we can incorporate them into our lives today:

1. The Law of Divine Oneness
2. The Law of Vibration
3. The Law of Action
4. The Law of Correspondence
5. The Law of Cause and Effect
6. The Law of Compensation
7. The Law of Attraction
8. The Law of Perpetual Transmutation of Energy
9. The Law of Relativity
10. The Law of Polarity
11. The Law of Rhythm

12. The Law of Gender

Let us discuss these laws to have a better understanding of them.

#1. Law of Divine Oneness

The first and fundamental law of the universe is known as the law of divine oneness. This law emphasizes the interconnected nature of all things. It states that beyond what our senses perceive, every thought, action, and event is intricately linked to everything else in some way. As a result, it is important to approach others with compassion and understanding, acknowledging that we are all interconnected and part of a unified whole.

#2. Law of Vibration

The law of vibration is considered one of the fundamental laws of the universe. It asserts that everything within the universe is in a constant state of movement, vibration, and circular motion. According to this law, all aspects of existence are perpetually in motion, and energy flows in waves and patterns. Furthermore, this law highlights the interconnected nature of all things, emphasizing that the energy we emit into the world is what we attract back into our own lives.

#3. Law of Action

The law of action, which stems from Sir Isaac Newton's Third Law of Motion, posits that for every action, there is an equal and opposite reaction. According to this law, when a force is exerted on an object, an equal and opposite force is exerted by the object in the opposite direction. In simple terms, when something pushes or acts upon an object, the object pushes back with an equal amount of force. This law emphasizes the balanced and reciprocal nature of forces in physical interactions.

#4. Law of Correspondence

The law of correspondence states that thoughts held in the conscious mind will create corresponding physical actions and events in the physical world. The law of correspondence states that "as within, so without," which means that what is happening in our internal world (thoughts, beliefs, and expectations) will be reflected in our external world (realities, experiences, and results).

#5. Law of Cause and Effect

The law of cause and effect is a principle that asserts that actions or events have consequences, and those consequences can be traced back to their initial causes. It states that for every cause, there is an effect, and for every effect, there is a cause.

It is important to recognize that every action we take will have a reaction, whether positive or negative. The energy and vibrations we emit into the world may not necessarily return to us immediately, but they create a ripple effect. If we project anger or resentment, for instance, it will eventually impact us in some way.

This law highlights the interconnectedness of our actions and their subsequent outcomes, reminding us to be mindful of the energy we put out into the world, as it can have lasting effects on ourselves and others.

#6. Law of Compensation

The law of compensation is a belief that suggests diligent work and dedication will be met with corresponding rewards. It states that the efforts we invest will ultimately be recognized and rewarded, whether through tangible benefits or intangible acknowledgments. According to this law, if we desire something, we must contribute and give something of value in return in order to move closer to our goals. It emphasizes the principle of reciprocity, where the energy and actions we put forth are mirrored in the outcomes we receive.

#7. Law of Attraction

The law of attraction is rooted in the belief that our thoughts, whether positive or negative, have the power to shape our experiences. It suggests that thoughts are composed of pure energy and that similar energy attracts similar energy. According to this principle, focusing on positive thoughts can lead to positive experiences, while dwelling on negative thoughts can bring about negative experiences. It emphasizes the importance of aligning our thoughts and beliefs with what we desire.

Merely repeating affirmations without genuine belief holds little value, according to this belief. The key is to focus on our desires rather than our fears and to have a genuine belief in the possibility of achieving what we seek. By consciously directing our thoughts and maintaining a positive mindset, we can attract and manifest the experiences and outcomes we desire in life.

#8. Law of Perpetual Transmutation of Energy

This law asserts that energy cannot be created or destroyed, but it can be transformed from one form to another. This principle aligns with the concept of energy conservation. It states that energy can be converted between different forms, such as from heat energy to electrical energy, while the total amount of energy in a system remains constant.

In the realm of human experiences, this law suggests that our thoughts hold significant power. Every action we take is preceded by a thought, and our thoughts have the potential to manifest in our physical reality. For instance, being around a negative person may affect our own positivity, leading to a depletion of our positive energy.

However, the law of perpetual transmutation of energy also highlights that higher frequencies can transmute lower ones when applied with intention. This means that positive and uplifting thoughts when consciously maintained, can transform and uplift negative energy around us.

With this understanding, we can actively choose to uplift the negative energy in our surroundings by cultivating positive thoughts and engaging in positive actions. By doing so, we contribute to the transformation and transmutation of energy, creating a more positive and harmonious environment.

#9. Law of Relativity

The law of relativity suggests that we have a tendency to

compare things in our world. However, in reality, every-thing is neutral, and meaning or value is subjective and dependent on our perception. If we find ourselves feeling un-grateful for our lifestyle, it could be because we are compar-ing our situation to someone else's perceived lifestyle. Instead, the advice is to focus on appreciating what we have because we may not fully understand or be aware of what others experience behind closed doors.

This concept highlights the importance of recognizing the relativity of our experiences and encourages us to cultivate gratitude for our own circumstances rather than constantly comparing ourselves to others. It serves as a reminder to be mindful of our perceptions and to appreciate the uniqueness of our own journey.

#10. Law of Polarity

The law of polarity states that within everything in life, there exists an opposite or contrasting aspect. This law recognizes that dualities are inherent in the world, such as good and evil, bravery and fear, and warmth and cold.

The key understanding of this law is that these opposites are interconnected and inseparable. They are like two sides of the same coin, and one cannot exist without the other.

Furthermore, the opposite side often contains the seed or essence of the original aspect. In other words, by exploring the opposite of something, we can gain deeper insights into its true nature.

For instance, understanding fear can provide a greater understanding of bravery, and understanding darkness can enhance our appreciation for light. This law encourages us to embrace the interplay of opposites and recognize that they contribute to the richness and complexity of life.

#11. The Law of Rhythm

The law of rhythm is a philosophical concept that suggests that all natural phenomena, including the universe itself, are governed by cycles of rhythm and repetition. It posits that everything in nature, regardless of its scale, experiences movement and interaction in rhythmic patterns.

This concept finds application in various aspects of life, both physical and metaphysical. For example, it helps explain the changing seasons, the cyclical phases of the moon, the cycles of birth and death, and the repeating patterns observed in history.

The law of rhythm emphasizes the inherent rhythmical nature of existence, highlighting that nothing remains static and that all things experience cycles of growth, transformation, decline, and renewal. It reflects the interconnectedness and harmony of the natural world and invites us to recognize and align ourselves with the rhythms and cycles that govern our lives.

#12. The Law of Gender

And lastly, the law of gender, as a philosophical concept, recognizes that all creation is composed of two opposing yet complementary energy forces: feminine and masculine. These energies exist and are expressed in both the spiritual and physical realms, playing an essential role in maintaining the balance of the universe. Gender, in this context, refers to the way in which these two forces interact and manifest in the physical world.

Understanding the law of gender allows us to perceive the interconnectedness of all things. It reveals that our actions and thoughts have an impact on the harmony of the universe. By acknowledging and embracing the interplay of feminine and masculine energies within ourselves and in the world around us, we can strive for a greater balance and alignment. This recognition prompts us to honor and respect the diverse expressions of gender and to appreciate the harmonious integration of these energies in our lives and in the universe.

Manifestation Power in Modern Science:

How Does It Work?

The manifestation power described in the previous chapter can be proven by experiments conducted in physics laboratories throughout the world today. These experiments prove that different states of consciousness (such as meditative states, sleep states, and altered states of consciousness) can produce different effects. In these experiments, a subject is placed in an electromagnetic field and then asked to enter a meditative state or an altered state of consciousness. The electromagnetic field that is used for these experiments has the capacity to manipulate the physical world by changing the electric and magnetic fields around it.

It is not just ancient human beings who have been trying to understand how manifestation power works in the physical universe for millennia. Modern science has also made a great effort at trying to comprehend this phenomenon as well.

The physical universe can be described as a manifestation of universal will. The physical universe is a reflection of the unmanifested that exists beyond it. As such, when we attempt to understand how the physical universe works, we are attempting to understand what happens in the unmanifested dimension as well.

Modern science has made great progress in understanding the physical universe and its workings through many discoveries that have been made throughout history. However, modern science has not made any progress towards understanding how human beings work and function in the physical world. In fact, modern scientific theories have only served to spread confusion because they are built on assumptions rather than solid evidence.

For instance, the belief that time is something that moves onward was invented by Western scientists in an effort to explain gravity. This idea was based on the observation that the planets in the solar system were moving in a straight line through space. This led scientists to propose that time itself was moving forward. This theory is now widely accepted by modern science, but it has no grounding in reality and only serves to give scientists an excuse for why they do not understand how the mind works.

Scientists have also made claims about how many things operate on the basis of quantum mechanics and wave functions. These theories are very similar to many of the ancient wisdom traditions that have described manifestation power as a function of consciousness. However, despite all their efforts, scientific experiments have not been able to confirm the predictions made by these theories.

The wisdom traditions that have included such advanced knowledge about manifestation power have only included it in their teachings as part of a larger intellectual understanding. They have not attempted to demonstrate this principle through experimentation. The fact that modern science still does not understand the workings of human consciousness clearly shows that it has not yet reached a stage where it is capable of understanding such a principle.

Our True Nature and Our Destiny

We are all manifestations of universal will, which can be described as an ocean of pure consciousness free from space and time but with infinite potential.

This means that all manifestations are pure consciousness, including the images we form in our minds when we think or make decisions.

This leads to the question of who we really are: Are we pure consciousness, or are we only what corresponds to our bodies and minds? The answer is that pure consciousness becomes manifest in a body and a mind through the process of creation but remains unchanged by the changes that occur in its manifestation. Pure consciousness is like an ocean of radiation and potential, which becomes manifest as rain when it falls into the earth. The earth absorbs all this rain and water and then becomes full due to this absorption. However, it is still nothing but water after it has absorbed all that rain.

It is important to understand that evolution, just like creation, is simply the manifestation of energy. This means that evolution is nothing but an attempt at understanding how energy manifests in the physical form.

Evolution describes the diversity of life on earth, and modern science has made great progress in understanding this process through many discoveries. However, it is possible that scientists are still not able to identify how life and consciousness function in a fully developed manifestation.

Because we are manifestations of universal will and have no foundation within our own consciousness, we must have a direct connection with that ocean of pure consciousness outside our minds. This means that we must be able to make a direct connection with the unmanifested dimension: outer space. This connection is reflected in deep meditation and altered states of consciousness.

It is a known fact that as we become more advanced in our meditation practice, our ability to communicate with the unconscious mind increases dramatically. At a certain level, no thoughts can enter our minds without our permission because they are reflections of reality in the form of energy waves.

Because we have no foundation within ourselves, we must have an unbroken connection to the unmanifested dimension outside our minds through meditation and altered states of consciousness. This means that only through these practices can we truly understand how universal manifestation works.

Evolution is the manifestation of energy, which can be

described as the unmanifested dimension.

It is a known fact that evolution does not happen by randomness alone or through chance It requires conscious intent to manifest. Evolution can also be described as "the evolution of physicality into consciousness."

Furthermore, all that exists in this universe are manifestations. Every manifestation reflects universal will in the form of energy waves because everything is made up of energy waves. The fact that there are many different types of energy waves connected with our planet and its environment does not mean that we are separate from the unmanifested dimension where all these energies originate and dissolve into themselves.

As we have seen, the sky is an image of consciousness in the same way that our thoughts are connected to consciousness. This means that when we look at it, all we are seeing is consciousness with no form. However, because of our limited vision, what we see outside is reflected in the form of energy waves.

This mirrors how our own mind works because all we can see within ourselves are reflections of unknown energies. We can only see these reflections due to the fact that our physical eyes reflect images outside in a very similar way as they reflect images inside.

This means that it is possible that the images we see in our mind are not forms of energy waves but a reflection of consciousness. Again, this does not mean we are separate from the universe; instead, it means that human consciousness must be able to create and dissolve these energies. This is what allows us to perceive images in our minds.

If this were not the case, then when we look at outer space, there would be no point in looking up at the sky or even looking out of a window. However, our ability to form ideas about reality based on these reflections of unknown energy waves allows us to use them as a tool for understanding the laws of manifestation.

The very same principle applies to all manifested forms. Every form is constantly being reabsorbed and recreated by the unmanifested dimension. This means that we are constantly creating new manifestations from nothing as we step into an altered state of consciousness.

Therefore, whatever occurs in a manifested form also occurs in one's own mind. Therefore, it is possible that whatever happens inside our mind also happens outside because this is how consciousness works.

It is impossible for us to know the workings of another form because we do not have access to them through the process of manifestation; therefore, it is possible that everything at a certain level of development will be like a mirror reflection of our own unconscious mind.

This principle can also be applied to evolution because it is the manifestation of energy, which originates from the un-manifested dimension. Therefore, a mutual reflection of our own unconscious mind can be perceived in the manifestations of nature.

However, this does not mean that matter has no physical existence. It simply means that it is possible for consciousness to manifest in physical forms and evolve over time. Therefore, it is possible for consciousness to undergo transformation through the process of evolution.

Evolving Consciousness

The process of evolution involves consciousness transforming from one state into another. This means that thoughts must be able to move at a speed faster than the speed of the universe in order for evolution to occur. This transformation can be described as a "passage through time."

As scientists have discovered, human consciousness can transform into information, which is an energy in the form of waves. If these waves are very dense and compact, then they can also travel through space at speeds faster than light. This process has been observed and recorded through observations of radio waves traveling at speeds faster than light and taking thousands of years to reach Earth.

In order for human consciousness to evolve, it must be able to move at a speed faster than the speed of the universe. This means that we must use this process of transformation and evolution to achieve a higher level of understanding.

This is why meditation can represent a bridge between the spiritual and physical realms by creating cycles within our minds that allow us to travel through time at faster speeds.

The only way our consciousness can be transformed into information is through meditation because there are no other ways in which human consciousness can become more advanced. Otherwise, if we had access to other abilities that did not involve meditation, then these abilities would also not require an increased level of understanding.

Our ability to meditate can be described as a higher form of intelligence because it allows us to maintain awareness of our conscious and unconscious mind in order to create a bridge between thought and the material realm.

However, meditation is not just for achieving an understanding of the laws of evolution. Our higher consciousness can also be used in order to affect physical reality.

The universe is a reflection of the underlying laws that allow everything inside it to exist from nothing. This means that if we want a change in what occurs within our own mind, then we need to learn how to manifest by changing ourselves into something more advanced through meditation.

The process of evolution can be depicted as a cycle that takes our consciousness from one stage to another. As we move through the cycle, our mind is constantly transforming in order to keep up with each new stage. Therefore, our consciousness is always moving through time and space at the speed of light.

This is why meditation can be described as a process that combines time and space. Meditation allows the thought processes within one's mind to replace old ideas with new ones. We do this through the process of replacing false beliefs with more advanced ones.

Time energy operates exactly like other types of energy because it allows us to create changes inside our reality. We can create these changes in a very short amount of time through meditation. This is why meditation is so important because it allows us to use the thoughts inside our mind and create new realities.

Magnetic Mental Contraction

According to science, our body contains a magnetic field that is positioned exactly at the center of our physical form. This means that we have the ability to reprogram our own brain by mentally contracting and expanding certain parts in order to concentrate or disperse other parts.

This is another way that human consciousness can become more advanced. We can give ourselves magnetic fields that allow us to direct thoughts into different areas of the brain and dilate them.

This technique can help us to get rid of false beliefs, attract higher levels of understanding, and direct our thoughts inside the brain. This is a complicated process because it requires us to concentrate on one part of our brain in order to direct another.

The problem is that there are no specific techniques that we can use in order to activate these magnetic fields within our own minds. If we find ourselves having difficulty using this technique, then it may be best for us to consult with a meditation instructor and learn from them the best methods for utilizing this process.

Through mental concentration, we have the ability to alter our consciousness and affect physical reality by creating friction between parts of our brains. This can involve concentrating on one part of our brain to the point that we can temporarily stop thinking. This allows us to enter a state of semiconsciousness and allows us to concentrate on other parts of our brains at the same time.

This is why meditation must involve a form of concentration in order for it to be used effectively. This involves the ability to control one's thoughts in order to slow down the process of time inside our own mind. Through this type of concentration, we can also direct certain sections within our brain so that we get rid of negative ideas, replace them with positive ones, and use these new beliefs as tools for improving reality.

The only way we can be able to use this technique is by being able to hold new ideologies in our minds for a certain amount of time. This is why meditation teachers must provide us with the ability to meditate and mentally focus our thoughts on one part of our brain for an extended period of time.

If we are not able to achieve this concentration, then we will not be able to use the process of mental contraction in order to change and improve ourselves. This is why some meditation teachers have created techniques that provide us with strategies for controlling our own brains by concentrating on only one section at a time.

It is very important for us to learn how to use our own brains so that we can direct our thoughts, update the material universe inside our minds, and be able to affect physical reality. We all must be able to control the force of time in order to create an improved version of ourselves. This is why meditators should also practice mental concentration on physical reality because it allows us to create a more advanced type of consciousness and train ourselves within this process.

Changing Time

One way that our minds can become more advanced is by changing time. We change time by changing our internal clock through meditation because this allows us to alter the entire material universe with our thoughts. Therefore, if we are continually changing our internal clock, then we can alter the entire material realm around us.

Through this technique, we can create more advanced realities inside our minds by utilizing time as a tool. This means that meditators can use their minds in order to alter the universe within their perception and alter the way they experience time.

We can accomplish this by using meditation to train our mind so that it has control over time. This is why meditation must involve a great deal of discipline in order for us to successfully use its powers.

One way to become more advanced is through the ability to control time. By altering our concept of time, we can also alter our perception of space and create a higher level of consciousness that allows us to control our own reality.

Through time, creatures have the ability to change their physical forms because time gives them the power to evolve and eventually become beings with superhuman powers. We have also experienced evolution due to a power known as Time.

A Yogi's Concept of Time

Yogis believe in the existence of an infinite amount of time within the material realm before the creation of man. This time, however, was formless and contained only within empty space. Through experiments, time gained the power to shape and transform space into physical matter. Consequently, the empty void within space transformed into a material world, and time and matter became inseparable.

Due to this understanding of time, Yogis place value not on material objects but rather on the process of their creation. This is why meditation holds great importance for Yogis, as it enables them to reactivate the creative process within their minds. Without meditation, Yogis would forget the process through which their own bodies were created. Thus, they engage in extensive meditation to remember the laws of nature and the process of self-creation, which helps them maintain their reality.

Yogis meditate extensively to retain the knowledge of how

their bodies were created and to establish a connection with their internal spirit and time itself. This connection empowers them to reach higher levels of development. Time is regarded by Yogis as a controlling spirit of universal existence, only accessible through physical experiences. Therefore, meditation and consciousness become crucial tools for Yogis to create their own reality and establish contact with time.

Through meditation, Yogis can re-experience the original creation process, aiding their understanding of the laws governing the physical body. The belief stems from the idea that time, as a spirit, possesses the ability to transform into physical matter. Eventually, all spiritual forces will merge with the material realm, uniting with it.

Ultimately, Yogis believe that all existence in the universe is created through time and controlled by a God who is part of all matter.

Yogis strive to attain time, the sole entity capable of transforming into physical matter. To achieve this, they diligently practice meditation to unlock psychic powers known as Siddhis, granting them extraordinary abilities. While numerous Siddhis can be acquired through meditation, only a select few are recognized for their capacity to alter conscious perception. The ethical application of these powers depends on the true intentions of the Yogi.

Among the crucial Siddhis sought by Yogis to transcend human limitations are clairvoyance, clairaudience, and teleportation. These abilities enable Yogis to explore their inner essence, necessitating their dedication to meditation. Through this practice, Yogis have gained psychic powers that enable them to access heightened realities and traverse alternate dimensions. By doing so, they concurrently exist on multiple planes of existence, comprehending the intricacies of creation and its purpose.

Time holds profound significance for Yogis as it represents the universal power from which the cosmos originated. As a force inseparable from physical matter, it necessitates Yogi's meditation to elevate consciousness and explore elevated realities. By establishing a connection with their inner spirit through meditation, Yogis commune with time, acquiring clairvoyance to comprehend the governing laws of the physical realm. This reinforces the notion that a divine entity through which the universe was created controls time.

This controlling force, referred to as an element or universal energy, permeates all life forms and facilitates the functioning of matter and energy within the material realm. The creation of time in its present state necessitates a dimension beyond the material, establishing a supernatural dimension. Through meditation, Yogis harness their ability to interact with this universal energy, becoming conduits for controlling forces.

Time's paramount significance to Yogis lies in its origin within their consciousness. Consequently, they possess the inherent power to comprehend its existence. Hence, their dedication to meditation facilitates an experiential understanding of higher realities and enhances their spiritual power.

Time and matter share an intrinsic connection, as both emanate from the same eternal spiritual force. This interconnecting energy system enables all universal existences to function seamlessly.

Hence, Yogis can advance their spiritual powers and gain a profound understanding of time and its existence. Their dedication to meditation serves as the gateway to unlocking these spiritual abilities. As elaborated in this chapter, Yogis establish communication with higher levels of reality by refining their spiritual powers.

What Is The Sacred Geometry of the Universe?

When it comes to comprehending the universe, many individuals solely focus on its physical aspect, limiting their understanding of the higher levels of existence. The inability to transcend the physical plane is often a result of being spiritually undeveloped and lacking knowledge of the universal laws of energy. To overcome this limitation, it is crucial for individuals to engage in meditation and enhance their spiritual abilities before delving into the workings of universal energy.

Through meditation, one can connect with higher realms of reality and strengthen their psychic abilities. By doing so, individuals gain insight into the laws of universal energy, enabling them to manipulate their consciousness and transcend the physical plane. This transcendence grants them a spiritual perception of time.

With spiritual advancement, individuals can gain a comprehensive understanding of universal energy and its composition. They acquire the power to shape their thoughts before entering different mental and emotional states. This deepened understanding allows them to enhance their spiritual abilities and explore higher levels of reality.

To comprehend the universe effectively, one must acknowledge that cosmic energy consists of three distinct forces. By separating into these forces, the universe can manifest a wide array of physical phenomena. Yogis have created diagrams, such as the sacred geometry of the universe, to illustrate the relationship between matter and two-dimensional space. These diagrams also depict how universal energy can exist as a four-dimensional entity that traverses through time.

Yogis realized that universal energy exists in various forms and can be better understood through the use of symbols. These symbols, including the seven-pointed star and the om, provide Yogis with profound insights into the interaction between universal energy and matter.

By delving into meditation and deepening their understanding of cosmic energy, Yogis grasped that everything in the universe is interconnected. They recognized the three fundamental aspects of God-Mind, which correspond to different facets of universal energy. These aspects include time and space, mastery over matter, and the reverse process of time. Yogis discovered that by harnessing their spiritual powers, they could manipulate time, interact with matter, and access higher levels of being.

Through their practice, Yogis acknowledged the impermanence of all things in the universe. They understood that everything undergoes a cycle of creation, destruction, and rebirth. This awareness contributed to their comprehension of the interconnectedness of all phenomena.

By developing techniques and utilizing their psychic abilities, Yogis gained the ability to control their minds and perceive the interconnectedness of all beings. They recognized that individuals communicate on various levels and that similarities between people are more significant than differences. Additionally, Yogis discovered that all beings possess a spiritual core and that humans are not the sole beings capable of perceiving it.

The practice of meditation and spiritual powers enabled Yogis to perceive the constant change in the world and transcend it. They realized that individuals are not static entities but are in a perpetual state of transformation. Yogis developed techniques to halt this continuous change and provide guidance to those seeking stability.

Yogis also understood that all beings, including humans and

animals, are equal parts of the universe. They could empathize with others by experiencing their thoughts and emotions firsthand. This deep connection allowed them to assist individuals who faced challenges.

Unlike others, Yogis did not perform these techniques as mere external practices but rather integrated them into their way of life, realizing that the true understanding of the universe lies within personal experience and transformation.

Wealth Manifestation

Have you ever wanted more money? You know what it can do for you: help your family live better or buy new things for yourself. How much would you be willing to earn?

Many people dream about having a big stash of wealth and leaving the world with them as they take flight in their private jet, but the truth is that no one will take care of them if they don't take care of themselves first. To build wealth, there are certain things you must do — like not accumulating debts and meditating on what it means to live and prosper in abundance every day while also investing your time intelligently.

Those are the simple yet very important steps that anyone can take to make money in their life. But not many people know that it is possible to achieve this since the popular perception of wealth is one of immense wealth and hence implies an absence of substance or probably even a lack of talent.

Nothing could be further from the truth: Real wealth comes from within you and through your efforts to promote an ideal lifestyle with practical pursuits. The key to success — and this is just a basic starting point — is having a belief that you can create abundance in your life and start living the way you want.

So, if you want to make money, you must realize that wealth is created through your thoughts and actions. Your life is the sum of your thoughts and actions. What you have become today is the result of your thoughts and actions yesterday. Money is a form of energy. Every action has an equal reaction. Every thought has a purpose or meaning to it. So everything we think and do matters, whether directly or indirectly, to what we receive in life — whether good or bad. The law of attraction governs human behavior in a great way that everyone should know about.

If you think and talk about many things in life but don't do much to make them happen, it makes no sense. It's because if you want to get something in your life, you must go for it vigorously. You must take the necessary steps to achieve what you want.

You might have the best intentions, but if your actions do not support those goals, what good are they? You must take action each day to bring your dreams alive. The more positive actions you take each day that promote your well-being and the well-being of others without expecting anything in return — as long as they are according to universal laws — the more positive effects will come back on you again.

Wealth is not a single concept. It's an attitude, a lifestyle that you choose to live, and the intention to make it happen in your life and the lives of those around you. We need to understand that we can create wealth through our actions and thoughts, just like we can create success through our actions and thoughts. Wealth manifests itself in our world, whether materially or not.

The world has so much garbage that we need to act upon in order to create a better world, and we should work towards doing so. We must understand the law of attraction is real, and it has an influence on everything we do. When you take action toward your dreams, you will attract more of those dreams into your life. Your view is the lens through which you interpret things and make choices — in other words, your beliefs — thus, the degree to which you attract things into your life is directly proportional to the degree to which you hold those specific beliefs about what's possible for you. The law of attraction works on the basis that if our thoughts are tied to positivity, it creates more positive situations or events. However, if our thoughts are tied to negativity, it creates more negative situations or events.

This is a basic starting point in understanding the law of attraction and how it works. You start becoming successful by getting into a flow with the things that you do each day. This can set the tone for what sort of energy flows through you. Think of your energy as a battery and your words and actions as the charger for that battery — whatever you do, say, or think affects not only your life but also the lives of others around you.

For example, if you want to be rich, start speaking about money as if it already exists in your life now — talk about it often and imagine yourself doing different things with all that money. Whenever you think of a situation where money could be useful, take action immediately to try and solve the problem.

Learn to use your energy in a positive manner so that you

can create positive results. If you want to do better in any-thing, it means you need to have the right attitude about things — without the right attitude, you will get nowhere. Just like when we say that something is a waste of time be-cause we are using it wrongly — the same thing goes with our lives. We could be using our time wisely each day, or we may be wasting it away without knowing it — which would be worse? It all depends on if we have the right attitude to-wards things in life or not.

The best way to understand the law of attraction is to apply it to your own life in order to create the results you want. When you begin to realize that your thoughts and actions do have the power to create what you want, then you will start taking action towards achieving those dreams of yours. This is step one — and at some point, it's not up for you anymore — so it's important that you work hard and make things happen for yourself by taking action every day.

Once you've created positive actions that support what you want, naturally, that's when things start coming back into your life as well. When you want the love of your life to yourself, you put yourself into a situation that creates the circumstances in which you will get what you want. You see, we can create our own reality by understanding the laws of attraction and doing things that create the circumstances in which we desire to live.

What we think and do each day affects every other thought and action that we take. But this is where our desires actually come from — so what exactly do they look like? You see, our minds are simply thoughts that create mental pictures of what we desire. It's basically just an image or a picture of what we hold in our minds as our desires — not only for other people but for ourselves as well.

You can change your mind, and you can change your life. But to do so, you must understand the power of thoughts and the law of attraction. When we desire things, we often create mental pictures of them in our minds — and it's from these thoughts that our desires flow from. This is how to build a vision board or use subconscious visualization to attract great wealth into your life — but it also applies to everything else you desire as well.

When we put ourselves into a certain situation, some people may choose to call this coincidence, luck, or fate — but it's all the same thing in the end. We often can't see past our own lack of understanding, but it's all the same thing in a way. You see, we are all the only ones who can create what is in our lives. We are the only ones who have control over what happens to us.

Whatever you put into your life, you will get out of it — this mantra applies to everything we do and think about doing. You must realize that everything is just a thought and be aware of these thoughts that flow through your mind each day — because if you don't know what you want, how can you ever hope to get it? Your thoughts create your present state of being. If you have the right thoughts, you will attract what you want into your life. So how do you get the right thoughts?

Every day, we are presented with opportunities to live our lives in a positive way — but we must realize that our own minds hold importance over these choices as well. In reality, each situation is a choice — and every choice has an outcome. The problem is that most people stay in situations that don't make them happy because they can't see past the circumstance they are already in. You must understand that it's OK to let go of things in order to attract things into your life.

For example, when you break up with your significant other, it may not seem like a good time to start dating someone else. But in reality, it's just the perfect time to start dating someone new if you are still not over the other person. If you don't make time for yourself and find somebody new, then that's when you'll start thinking about the old person all over again. Breakups are often said to be the best times in a relationship — because now you have completely cut off all outside factors in your life that prevented you from focusing on yourself.

Staying in a situation that doesn't make you happy may not be the best decision, but staying in it just because it is "the way things are" causes a lot of unnecessary suffering. This is the principle of never giving up on your goals and dreams. You must realize that there's always an easier way out of most situations, and if you can see past the circumstances yourself, then you will find it every time. How do you know when to act on what you want?

When something doesn't make sense to us anymore, this means we're getting exhausted by all these things that don't make sense. We must see past everything and see what opportunities arise for us going forward. Don't be afraid to leave situations that cause you a lot of stress and don't allow you to live your dreams. When things start getting hard, your positive thinking will be tested — but in reality, this is the perfect time to find new opportunities.

Think positive, and everything will fall into place — because our thoughts are all we have. To create what we want in life and make our desires come true, we must realize that we always have control over our own thoughts and actions. We must focus on the reality of today instead of being stuck on a past or future situation that may never happen again. We must know that our minds hold tremendous power over everything in life.

The Role of Meditation in
Wealth Manifestation

If you want to know the truth about why some people have abundance, and others don't, it boils down to a simple question: who are you spending time with? The same principle applies as it relates to wealth.

You are not alone in feeling like your life lacks something, or you find yourself in situations where you're an observer rather than an active participant. It's natural for this feeling of emptiness or lack to bother us, but we can use meditation as a tool to transform how we respond and manifest greater degrees of satisfaction and well-being.

Meditation is not merely sitting in the lotus position with our eyes closed (although, yes, there is such a thing!). It is a practice that involves training your mind to be more responsive and flexible in how you respond to the world around you. It shifts our perception from reactionary to responsive, from suffering to a state of joy, contentment, and ease.

When we are able to look at situations not as problems or barriers but as opportunities for growth and learning, we relax into a whole new level of consciousness. The ego-driven self takes a back seat, allowing the greatest self — the true self — to emerge in its place. We begin to awaken to our innate capacity for love and connection with others, with ourselves, and with the world at large.

The primary function of meditation is to clear the mind through techniques that involve breathing, visualization, and focusing on an object in the mind's eye. It is about training our mind to respond rather than react, and so the process involves becoming aware of the chatter in our mind, identifying it for what it is — unwanted thoughts — and letting them go. We learn to observe the thoughts in our mind without judging them, just as we would look at clouds moving across the sky without thinking anything of it.

Meditation is far more than simply sitting silently and breathing in and out. It is a practice that can be used to address a wide range of issues, from anxiety and depression to physical pain and anything else causing suffering. Because our mind is so powerful, once we train it to respond rather than react — and we all have that capacity within us — we are then able to transcend our personal limitations and experience greater degrees of freedom.

When we are able to look at situations not as problems or barriers but as opportunities for growth and learning, we relax into a whole new level of consciousness. The ego-driven self takes a back seat, allowing the greatest self — the true self — to emerge in its place. We begin to awaken to our innate capacity for love and connection with others, with ourselves, and with the world at large.

The Secret of the Soul by Samael Aun Weor Meditation starts with the recognition that a person is a soul and not an animal, specifically a human being. It begins with the recognition that everything exists in a continuous state of change and equilibrium between opposites – hot as cold, light as dark, or positive as negative. Meditation teaches us how to maintain this equilibrium, which means adopting the attitude of tolerance towards everything that occurs in life, good or bad. This is not a passive attitude but rather an active and dynamic one. By nature, man is a positive being, and as such, he resists nothing, neither pain nor pleasure.

To know that our soul has its own life and identity apart from its physical body, we have to develop a capacity to distinguish the two with total freedom. When we clearly recognize that our physical body is only the vehicle through which we manifest ourselves on earth and that the soul has its own life within us, we begin to live the ideal existence of a human being: complete with thoughts and emotions, good or bad; in peace or in pain; happy or sad or anywhere in between.

One primary benefit of meditation is that it helps us develop a healthy relationship with our present environment and surroundings. When we feel at home, we can better enjoy the beauty of nature, appreciate the good things that happen to us, and overcome our fears and anxieties. When we feel alienated from our surroundings, we may react in ways that are detrimental to ourselves and others around us. We may become unappreciative of the beauty around us or miss out on opportunities that would have made life more enjoyable.

Being a positive person who lives by his own set of standards is a prerequisite for being able to practice meditation effectively or in the right way. We have to have enough self-esteem to feel and accept whatever happens in life without feeling sad, victimized, or angry. It is through this attitude of acceptance that we open ourselves up to greater possibilities.

When we practice meditation, we are actually training our minds to think subliminally. This means that our thoughts become more positive and constructive and contrary to the negative thought patterns of the past. We go from a reactive state—which is the result of our mind's habit of creating problems out of everything it sees as negative—to a more receptive and proactive state, which gives us the capacity to live in peace and harmony with ourselves, others and even the world around us.

If we learn to breathe meditatively, then the mind automatically brings about a change within us that allows our thoughts to become positive and constructive. In other words, our thoughts begin to obey us rather than us obeying them. Mystics and teachers of every age have talked about what they called the "still small voice" or "the voice of conscience," which tells people how they should live their life or what they should do to improve themselves. We all hear it, but we need to improve ourselves so that it becomes clear and distinct, something we can no longer ignore but must acknowledge. Meditation is a way of learning to hear it.

Buddhism is a very suitable practice for anyone who wants to live a more conscious and healthier life. Meditation for Buddhists is about practicing self-discipline, learning to detach from all kinds of conditions that are disruptive to our well-being, and learning to subjugate the mind so that we can experience states of higher consciousness. It is a practice that develops our intellect and elevates us spiritually. Still, this kind of meditation is different from that which can be practiced by Westerners. We're not using the mind to try to change ourselves or improve our mental state; instead, we're using it to better understand life and find peace within us.

Since most of us want to live in harmony with others and with nature as well, this kind of practice makes sense for anyone seeking a healthier, more peaceful, and more fulfilling existence on Earth. Meditation helps us overcome our fears, anxieties, and traumas that have accumulated over the years through the process of imprinting them within the unconscious mind. When we learn to meditate properly, these things are taken care of naturally, leaving us with a feeling of inner peace. The most important characteristic of this kind of meditation is that it's an active process and not just one where we sit back and let someone else do the work for us. Meditation is a process where we assume total responsibility for ourselves and our lives. It is a way of learning to trust in a higher power by taking responsibility for our own lives. It is a way of finding peace within ourselves and learning to live in harmony with life.

The purpose of meditation is to help us understand how we function on a deeper level and how we function in the realm of thoughts, emotions, and even subconscious beliefs. Meditation helps us deal with our problems in a very healthy way and develop an attitude that allows us to see things from new perspectives. It helps us become more cognizant of the fact that life is full of challenges but also full of possibilities for growth, happiness, and contentment. When we practice meditation and get in touch with our spiritual side, we begin to understand the role and importance of prayer in our lives. Everything that happens in life is a kind of prayer. We begin to realize that whatever happens to us is actually good for us because it gives us a chance to grow as humans. Life becomes something beautiful and worthwhile when we live it that way.

Buddhism teaches us about a number of things, including karma, reincarnation, compassion for all beings on earth, and other aspects related to the concept of an enlightened way of life.

I'm not a religious person because I believe that religion is a way of organizing human beings so that they can live in peace and harmony with each other. There's nothing wrong with that, but I don't think it's necessary to organize people around an ideology that says there is an actual God outside of our own understanding who can intervene in every aspect of our lives. People don't want to be told how to live their lives by others in that kind of way because it doesn't allow for the freedom most human beings need. Most people want to be responsible for themselves and their own thoughts and feelings.

There are four realizations that open up when we practice meditation:

1. We shed light on the fact that everything is not permanent. We begin to see things for what they are, not as good or bad things that are permanent. We begin to understand that life is a process of learning, and we must keep learning if we want to preserve our peace and happiness.

2. We begin to recognize that there is an innate self-awareness within us that helps us understand who we are and what we can become, although it's not

always easy at first to realize this.

3. We begin to realize that the external object (the universe) and the internal object (ourselves) can be treated in the same way. We shed light on what we call "the external object," which is really nothing more than a manifestation of our own inner essence. We realize that there's nothing outside of us but rather our own way of being and thinking within ourselves.

4. We begin to recognize how important it is for us to work on ourselves so that we not only build up but also maintain a relationship with our higher self because no one else can do this for us. In the process of doing so, we begin to understand that there is another way of life that is more fulfilling and satisfying than the one we have been living in our physical existence. In the course of time, we learn everything we need to know about this path in order to lead a happy and peaceful life.

I believe that meditation helps us free ourselves from all kinds of masks and appearances which obscure our natural state as beings who are essentially pure in nature. We shed light on the fact that there's only one thing in this world-pure existence. That's why it's important for us to practice meditation because it helps us shed light on the very essence of being human.

That's the way I look at meditation.

Because I believe that there is nothing outside of the universe, everything we do becomes a kind of prayer. Life becomes truly and completely meaningful when we do everything for the purpose of manifesting our pure essence, our higher self. We become whole and complete as human beings when we live according to this kind of philosophy. So I think meditation is something that everyone should experience because it gives us a sense of peace and enlightenment that no one else can give us. It is also very important for people to be able to recognize how free they can be if they live in harmony with themselves by following their hearts' desires.

Meditation is just one part of the process of living in harmony with our own being. I don't think we should ever be afraid of learning something new and challenging if we want to live a more meaningful life. And the more we practice meditation, the better it will become for us.

I know people who are very interested in meditation who think that it's too difficult or takes a long time before they get results from this kind of practice, but that's not the case at all. In fact, the more you do it, the better it gets. I believe that if we work on ourselves and abandon those thoughts and ideas that would keep us from progressing in life, then meditation becomes a much more profound practice.

There's no shortcut to success in life because each of us is unique. It's very important to understand this and accept the fact that what we do must be done in accordance with our own needs and ways of being. We can never achieve perfection with meditation because there is always something new to learn. We begin to understand that we can never really become perfect human beings, but it's important for us to learn how to develop ourselves so that we can live a more satisfactory and meaningful life. Meditation is what helps us do this.

The best way to meditate is by becoming one with yourself. You have to be willing to let go of what you have been thinking and feeling in the past and embrace your own inner self. The process of doing so takes time, patience, effort, and self-confidence. But if you really want something in life, then you have to be willing to make sacrifices if necessary.

If someone tells you that they're going to marry you because they think it's a good idea or because they want something from you, but they don't really love you as much as they say they do, then be willing to walk away from them. Don't give in too easily or allow yourself to get sucked into their world. If we allow people to take control of our lives and make decisions about our futures for us, then we can't really be happy. We are what we do, not what we say. The greatest self-confidence is being able to let go of everything that binds us to the external world and letting our pure essence live free in harmony with nature.

Everything in life becomes a kind of prayer when you become one with yourself. When you do this, then all objects dissolve into their very essence, and we begin to realize that there's no difference between an apple tree growing in a forest and the universe itself. Meditation helps us learn how to get in touch with the essence of everything and everyone, and that's what brings us happiness and peace.

25 Ways on How to Manifest Positive Energy in Order to Bring Wealth into Your Life

Manifesting positive energy involves attracting good vibes and cultivating inner peace. It goes beyond simply creating a more "positive" life in the conventional sense and focuses on enhancing overall well-being.

There are various approaches to manifesting positive energy. Some individuals prefer meditation as a manifestation tool, while others find solace in nature walks that help them connect with their future selves. Practices like yoga and maintaining a healthy diet can also contribute to the manifestation of positive energy.

Regardless of the chosen method, the key is to discover what resonates with you personally and to consistently incorporate it into your routine. Remember, there are numerous ways to manifest positive energy. The following 25 tips can be helpful:

#1. Release Negative Energy through Creative Outlets:

Take deep breaths, holding each breath for 10 seconds before exhaling slowly. Repeat this three times to relax your heart and ease stress. Engage in activities like writing, singing, or creating art to channel negative emotions into something positive.

#2. Visualize Your Desires:

Clearly visualize what you want to achieve, focusing on the details. Create a vision board with images and affirmations that inspire and motivate you. Review your vision board regularly to keep your goals in mind.

#3. Practice Gratitude:

Express gratitude for the good things in your life, no matter how small. Maintain a gratitude journal to cultivate a positive mindset and shift your focus towards positive thoughts.

#4. Maintain a Positive Outlook:

Avoid negative thoughts and emotions. When negativity arises, take a deep breath and redirect your attention to positive subjects. Start each day with a smile, cultivate optimism, and let positive vibes flow.

#5. Believe in Yourself:

Have faith in your abilities and believe that you can achieve your goals. Remind yourself of past successes and accomplishments to boost self-confidence.

#6. Let Go of the Past:

Forgive yourself for your mistakes and let go of negative emotions that hold you back. Focus on the present moment and embrace positive energy.

#7. Be Open to Change:

Embrace new possibilities and be open to positive changes in your life. Step outside your comfort zone and explore new opportunities.

#8. Practice Patience:

Manifesting positive energy takes time, so be patient. Trust that the universe is working in your favor, and keep faith in the process.

#9. Take Action:

While being patient, take small, consistent steps toward

your goals. Actively pursue actions that align with your desires and have faith that they will lead to positive results.

#10. Appreciate What You Have:

Be grateful for the blessings and positive aspects of your life. Acknowledge and appreciate the good things you already possess.

#11. Surround Yourself with Positive People:

Spend time with supportive and optimistic individuals who understand and encourage your goals. Surrounding yourself with positive influences will amplify your positive energy.

#12. Trust Your Intuition:

Listen to your inner voice and trust your intuition. Develop a connection with your higher self and follow its guidance toward positive outcomes.

#13. Meditate:

Engage in regular meditation to quiet the mind, connect with your higher self, and tap into a more positive frequency. It helps you manifest your goals and maintain a positive state of being.

#14. Connect with Nature:

Spend time outdoors, whether it's walking in a park, hiking, or simply sitting among trees. Nature grounds you and fills you with positive energy.

#15. Engage in Activities You Love:

Participate in activities that bring you joy and make you feel in the flow. When you enjoy what you do, positive energy naturally follows.

#16. Let Go of Control:

Release the need to control every aspect of your life. Embrace the unknown and be open to new possibilities and opportunities.

#17. Practice Self-Kindness:

Treat yourself with compassion and understanding. Take care of your mental health and forgive yourself for mistakes. Being kind to yourself helps attract positive energy.

#18. Be Kind to Others:

Extend kindness and compassion to others. Treating others with respect and positivity creates a ripple effect of positive energy.

#19. Smile:

Smiling is a simple yet powerful way to manifest positive energy. It uplifts your mood and sends a message of happiness and goodwill.

#20. Spread Joy:

Make it your mission to bring joy to others through kind words, deeds, or acts of generosity. Spreading joy not only makes others happy but also attracts positive energy into your life.

#21. Decrease Social Media Time:

Limit your exposure to negative influences on social media. Unfollow accounts that bring negativity and consciously curate your online experience to focus on positivity.

#22. Use Affirmations Daily:

Repeat positive affirmations that align with your goals and desires. Affirmations help shift your thought patterns and attract positive energy.

#23. Practice Self-Love:

Take care of yourself emotionally and physically. Prioritize self-care, get enough rest, eat nourishing food, exercise, and engage in activities that bring you joy.

#24. Establish a Morning Routine:

Create a morning routine that sets a positive tone for your day. Include activities like meditation, journaling, affirmations, or exercise to center yourself and start the day on a positive note.

#25. Be Truthful:

Be honest with yourself and others. Stay aligned with your authentic self, as truthfulness promotes positivity and attracts positive energy.

By incorporating these practices into your life consistently, you can cultivate a positive mindset, manifest positive energy, and attract positive outcomes.

Is Manifesting a Sin?

(Plus 10 More Questions Answered)

Is Manifesting a Person Bad?

It is not wrong to wish for something that you like – but think about it. Think more deeply, especially if it has to do with another person. The other person has their own freedom. They have the right to command their own life.

So, if you manifest that person in your life, the just way is to have them decide if they want to stay with you the way you want them to. If you start controlling what they do, that is a form of witchcraft.

Manifesting the person by taking away the control they have over their life is terrible. Using positive thinking and attitude to attract a person to your life is another thing.

So, you should never mess when anyone's independence if

ever you find yourself leaning towards Manifestation.

Why Do Some Christian People Believe Manifesting and the Law of Attraction Are Bad?

So, you've looked at some manifestation resources. You cannot believe that they could be anything but good. If the result is good, what do you have to complain about?

However, sometimes when you ask for things without making them in Jesus Christ's name, you attract the wrong kind of energy. You may think that you are connecting to yourself, but you may be connecting to something closer to witchcraft.

Calling upon something else other than Jesus Christ is going against God's plan.

Okay, even if you are not Christian and do not believe in the Bible, think about it. When you put a wish out there, do you always think that it is always something good that will connect with you?

Christian teachings involve sacrifice and long-suffering. The Bible has people like Job going through so many trials but still praising God in the end.

Yes, even if everything seems successful on the outside, getting your way more quickly can take away the sacrifice from you. You can get too used to getting whatever you want when you want it.

Do you remember the Parable of the Talents? The ones who worked hard towards their goal were the ones who were rewarded. Jesus Christ also taught people to ask for what they need: "Give us this day, our daily bread..."

So, it does not seem bad to ask for good things. However, you should always keep your intentions in check.

Are you doing it to be better than everyone else?

Are you doing it for revenge?

Are you doing it because you want the easy way out?

If you say yes to one or all of the three questions above, you are in danger of making manifestation a bad thing.

What qualifies as a sin, anyway?

At this point, we know that manifestation can lead you to a prideful existence. It can make you greedy for more since you have been told that you can get whatever you want if you let it.

Is Manifestation Dangerous?

Some people believe that manifestation is dangerous because it exposes you to a certain degree of meditation. It is when you let your guard down and open yourself out.

Sometimes when you do this, not in prayer but wishing for what you want, you end up summoning something else. It will definitely not be God – but something else, a darker power.

Calling someone to help you and directing it to the universe makes it prone to getting answered by other powers. They will not be powers that you want to be taking notice of at all.

Is Manifesting Against Religion?

It will have to depend on the religion. Christianity warns against the dangers of falling into the trap of manifestation.

Christians also believe that meditation should be done only for religious purposes. For them, it should only be used to call upon God and to connect with him.

Religion teaches us patience and understanding. Manifestation teaches us the opposite, which is of taking it upon yourself to get what you want.

It can be a tricky rope because praying for something can become more intense. You need to watch how much you desire something.

If it is peace of mind and better mental health that you need, your healing does not have to be wholly religious. It is actually safer to consult a therapist instead of letting the universe take action.

Is Manifesting the Devil's Work?

Christians believe that manifesting is a sly way the Devil is working towards good people. It is a way for you to think that whatever you are doing is actually good, but it is not.

You are being asked to communicate with the universe because it seems easier to accept that. In fact, you are connecting to the world.

It sounds a lot worse when you are connecting with the world. It spells it out for you: "worldly."

Satan tempted Jesus Christ with the world's riches if he would bow down and worship him. Jesus set an example by repeatedly saying no. The Christian faith is about taking the road less traveled instead of taking the smoother path.

Wrap-Up

So, is manifestation a sin?

On its own, it does not seem to be. After all, it cannot be that different from a little bit of daydreaming, does it? You simply focus on the things you want and work hard for them.

Calling on another power and going against the commandments of the church is what makes manifestation a sin.

Manifestation Is Not Magic

Manifestation is not magic. It is the process of aligning your thoughts, emotions, and actions with your desired outcome.

The first step is to get clear about what you want. This requires some serious introspection and self-awareness. What do you really want in life? What are your deepest desires? Once you have a good understanding of what you want, you can begin to take steps to manifest it.

The next step is to focus your attention on your desire. This means keeping your mind focused on what you want and visualizing it as if it has already happened. See yourself living your dream life, and feel the emotions that come with it.

The final step is to take action. This is where many people get stuck because they think that manifestation is all about visualization and positive thinking. However, you also need to take action towards your goals. This might mean making some changes in your life or taking some risks. Whatever it is, don't be afraid to take that first step.

Manifestation is not magic, but it is a powerful process that can help you create the life you want. Just remember to focus on what you want, visualize it, and take action.

The better you get at aligning your energy with your desired outcome, the faster you will see results. The key is to trust the process and have faith that what you desire is on its way.

Here are a few tips to help you align your energy for manifestation:

#1. Get clear on what you want.

The first step is to get clear on what you desire. What is your heart's deepest desire?

Get in touch with your feelings and allow yourself to dream big.

#2. Raise your vibration.

In order to attract what you desire, you must raise your vibration.

This can be done by meditating, practicing gratitude, and doing things that make you feel good.

#3. Take an aligned action.

After you have raised your vibration, it is important to take aligned action steps toward your desired outcome.

This means taking actions that are in alignment with your goal.

#4. Let go of the outcome.

One of the most important things to remember is to let go of attachment to the outcome.

Trust that what you desire is on its way, and have faith in the process.

Meditation Techniques for

Wealth Manifestation

Meditation has been used for centuries by spiritual and religious communities as a way to connect with their inner selves and divine energy. Recently, this practice has also gained popularity in everyday research, with scientists attributing its effects to increased focus, mental clarity, emotional balance, and more fulfilling sleep. If you want to improve your wealth manifestation practices through meditation on an individual level or if you're curious about what the most effective techniques are in general, then this chapter is for you!

In today's digital age, where we never seem to be able to get away from work or our responsibilities "in real life," the convenience of connecting with ourselves through technology is becoming more apparent. Over the last decade, meditation apps have been created for absolutely any kind of user. These range from apps that tell you how to meditate to apps that offer guided meditation sessions to meditation apps designed for children. One app even claims to be able to help users meditate in eight weeks by playing the sounds of chirping birds and ocean waves (that last one made me chuckle). Having gone through a phase where I tried almost every app available, I am now back to my regular practice of just sitting and closing my eyes.

For those of you who are at the beginning stages of developing your meditation practices, I highly recommend starting with the app Headspace. This app takes a unique approach to meditation by segmenting your practice into ten-minute sessions. Each session includes a warm-up exercise and then asks you to focus on one aspect of meditation, such as observing thoughts in your head without engaging with them or counting your breaths. These games are extremely simple and can easily be transferred into regular practice once you've reached the end of the ten-minute session. The app itself is free, but it can be more personalized if you choose to pay for it.

For those of you who are more experienced with meditation and interested in how to improve your wealth manifestation practice through this essential practice, here are some tips and techniques that I've found to be effective over the years:

1. **Start with a short duration:** There's no need to overwhelm yourself with a thirty-minute session straight away. If you're just starting out, start with a very short amount of time, say three minutes or even one minute. In fact, over the last week, I have been practicing meditation for less than twenty seconds at a time. As you continue developing your skills, gradually increase the length of time until you feel satisfied with your ability to focus for longer periods of time.

2. **Give it your full attention:** Even if you're not in a particularly busy work schedule, chances are you will often be thinking about something during your meditation practice. Thoughts run through our minds so quickly that we rarely notice them until we stop and reflect upon them for just a few moments. The good news is that the thoughts themselves don't matter because they don't impact our well-being or life path in any manner. However, when you do notice those pesky thoughts and choose to engage with them (whether it's to stop yourself from drifting off into sleep or an argument with your partner), this can

cause your practice to be less effective than it could be otherwise.

3. **Breathe deeply:** When done correctly, proper breathing is essential for developing a clear and conscious mind. Incorrect breathing can reduce the level of focus you have during your practice as well as cause other physical ailments in your body. The way to correct this is to breathe in through your nose and out through your mouth, making sure you are extending your inhale (which should last four seconds) and exhale (which should last eight seconds). It's best to find a place where you can sit down comfortably in order to focus on your breath instead of trying this while standing up or sitting on a bus or train to get to work.

4. **Think about your problems:** During my first attempts at meditation, I would often find myself thinking about impossible problems and worries that I had no control over. Whether it was my lack of motivation to clean the kitchen or my fear of not being able to pay off student loans, these thoughts would frequently cause stress, which ultimately made me more anxious and stressed out than before. It took a while until I knew that this "problem meditation" is an actual thing (especially since every person's mental health is

different). If you are like me and find that your practice of sitting down and closing your eyes makes you think about the things in life you don't want to think about, then try focusing on how grateful you are for the things in your life instead. In time, you can learn to focus on the positive things in your life that bring you peace and happiness.

5. **Find a mantra or affirmation:** If you're like most people who start off on their meditation practice, everything will seem new and strange, especially if you've never done it before. If your session invariably feels awkward and even pointless, try finding a mantra or affirmation to direct your thoughts towards during this time. This could be, "I am wealthy," or "I do not chase; I attract wealth in my life." Keep this mantra or affirmation in mind during your entire practice, even if you find yourself drifting away from it with other thoughts.

6. **Allow your mind to wander:** During your meditation session, you will probably notice that your attention keeps wandering back to things that interest you in the moment. This is natural and a sign that you are improving (however marginally). Instead of being upset at this, welcome these thoughts and let them

flow through the stream of your consciousness. It may help to think about how a river carries loads of different things without getting overwhelmed by them. The same happens with our minds when we meditate. Instead of being frustrated by the fact that our mind can't be still, we should embrace the fact that it is constantly changing and provides us with opportunities to change ourselves and learn new things.

These are some tips to help you meditate more effectively: acknowledge what meditation is (a practice with tangible benefits) and why you want to do it.

Manifesting Money Using the Law of Attraction for Financial Abundance

Everyone desires to accumulate more wealth, make more money, and live an abundant life. However, many people struggle with manifesting money and wealth due to their negative relationship with money. The key factor holding them back is their belief system regarding money.

To effectively change your beliefs about money and open yourself up to prosperity, leveraging the law of attraction is crucial. But before you can witness its transformative power, you need to take certain steps.

#1. Identify and change limiting beliefs about money

To activate the law of attraction in your life, it's important to identify and address any limiting beliefs you hold about money. These beliefs are often internalized over time and can hinder your financial success. Examples of such beliefs include thinking that money is hard to acquire, money can't buy happiness, or being wealthy conflicts with being a good person.

By recognizing these limiting beliefs and reframing them, you can develop a mindset that acknowledges money as an accessible and unlimited resource. Positive affirmations are a powerful tool for addressing these beliefs. For instance, you can affirm, "I am a money magnet. Everything I touch turns to gold," or "I release negative thoughts and emotions about money and visualize my dreams freely." What you repeatedly tell yourself becomes your reality, so using positive affirmations can help you develop a mindset conducive to attracting wealth.

#2. Visualize your wealth as if you've already achieved it

According to the Law of Attraction, what you believe inwardly and project outwardly determines what you attract into your life. To attract money, it's essential to visualize yourself already possessing it.

Visualizing a world where you have the wealth you desire not only fosters a receptive mindset for financial gain but also fuels your motivation to keep pushing forward. This visualization allows you to imagine your life after achieving your financial goals. Additionally, it cultivates an abundance mindset rather than a scarcity mindset.

The wealthy are often able to accumulate more wealth because they view money as abundant and attainable. They also see their existing money as a tool for generating more rather than something to protect or hoard. By visualizing money as something you already have in abundance, you can develop this abundance mindset. For a tangible reminder, carry a hundred-dollar bill in your pocket, which can make you feel wealthier and prevent a mindset of being broke.

#3. Cultivate gratitude and trust in the universe

Never underestimate the power of gratitude when it comes to manifesting money and opportunities. The universe tends to provide more of what you are genuinely grateful for.

Expressing gratitude not only fuels your passion but also eliminates limiting beliefs, making you more receptive to new opportunities. As you adopt a positive mindset regarding money and leverage the law of attraction, remember to practice gratitude.

Be thankful for the money you currently have, every

opportunity to make more money and the moments when those opportunities pay off. Regardless of your current income, maintaining an attitude of gratitude is essential for attracting more abundance into your life.

Importance of a Positive Mindset and Focus

A positive mindset is more than focus and determination - it's a feeling of satisfaction and general happiness with life. It can be challenging to maintain this positivity, but with a few tips, you'll be able to do so. By following these five simple steps, you'll develop an even greater understanding of this subject that can benefit your life in many ways.

1. Wear a smile
2. Live in the moment
3. Imagine the best possible outcome for every situation
4. Take time off
5. Take advantage of any positive opportunity

If you want to be happy, then start by looking for things that make you happy. When you're in the midst of a catastrophic problem, it's difficult to think objectively about your situation and how to solve it. It's not possible to think positively when negative thoughts overwhelm your thoughts. It's impossible. At any moment, however, you can commit yourself to a more positive mindset by thinking about what makes you feel good and doing more of that. Even at its worst, the world is still full of amazing people and remarkable experiences waiting for you to discover them. The most important thing you can do is to make it your goal to take the time and make an effort to look for them.

If you want to know how to build a successful business, what kind of food you should eat, who you should date, or how to really make money working from home, this doesn't require some magical approach that's not possible for most people. You probably already have ideas about what would eventually work and fail for you - but that doesn't mean that there's not more that you can do or learn from. Even if there isn't, at least it will give you something constructive to think about during those times when your mind builds up negative thoughts, and your life seems unendingly bleak. As long as you're not actively thinking about the problems you're facing, you can be working towards a solution and developing a more positive mindset. This will give you that much more time to think of your own success story and the ways in which you can continually make things better.

When your thoughts are focused on anger, resentment, desperation, or any of the other emotions commonly accompanied by negative thinking, it becomes extremely difficult to think about anything else. What's worse is that this type of mindset is almost always self-defeating and leads to nothing but feelings of failure and inadequacy. As long as you can remember to focus on the positive, however, there's no reason why your life can't become better every day. No matter how hard it can seem, you can find ways to adapt yourself to new ideas and thoughts that will help you see things in a more positive manner.

As long as you're living, there's always the chance that you'll find something new and exciting in your life. As soon as you start taking time off for yourself or relaxing after a long day of work, however, it's important that you commit to your own happiness. Take time off to do the things that make you happy - whether it's spending time with loved ones or going on a vacation - and remember to think positively about everything around you. With a positive mindset, there are many more opportunities to enjoy life and develop friendships with the people around us.

As long as there are good things in life, you can make it better. If you're constantly focusing on the negative things in your life, however, then you may never see the good things coming to you - and that's a shame. Aside from those times when you absolutely have to take action and take on a project, there are also many other opportunities to develop a positive mindset that will help you become happier every day. This isn't just about making yourself feel better about your work or even about your life - it's about making yourself feel alive. Life has too much potential for us to give up all hope of feeling happy. This isn't just something you can promise yourself - you can make it happen. When you're feeling stressed out, overwhelmed, or just plain tired, it's important that you take the time to realize that your situation is temporary.

As long as there are reasons for you to feel happy and hopeful, then there's a chance for positive change in your life. Even when things seem bleak, therefore, there's no reason why things couldn't get better with some extra effort and attention to your health. You'll probably never be fully prepared for what happens in life - but if you consider yourself a better person because of it, then it was all worth the time and effort after all.

It's not always easy to have a positive mindset, but you should make it your goal to keep things positive. Even when you're not feeling up to par or when life feels just overwhelmingly difficult, there's always a chance that things can get better if you take the necessary action.

At the end of the day, even when we are feeling down and like nothing will ever be good again - we must remind ourselves that we are alive and appreciate everything around us. Even the worst situations in life can be overcome with a positive mindset and sometimes by just taking a breath of fresh air.

If you want to be happy, then it's important to start looking for reasons to be happy. This doesn't have to be something that you do as a conscious effort - but as a lifelong commitment. Even when things seem impossible, and you're not sure why you're doing it anymore, there's still a chance that things could get better with effort and perseverance.

If you want to be successful in life, then it's quite important for you to maintain a positive mindset. This doesn't mean that you have to constantly think positive thoughts - it just means that you should always be thinking positively and taking positive action. Even the most difficult times in life will eventually pass, but the times when you are in control of your mindset are the ones that matter.

At some point in your life, you'll probably experience something that makes you believe that there is more to life than what you're currently experiencing. At some point during your life, it's possible for relationships to end abruptly and for things to feel hopeless for a while. It's also important for you to realize that these are temporary situations, even if they feel like they're forever sometimes.

When suddenly life seems to stagnate, you can take action, take charge and change things for the better. When you spot you're down in the dumps; there's never a reason why things can't get better over time.

If you're having a tough time coping with an opportunity or situation in your life, there's always something that you can do to help yourself and make things better. Even when we least expect it, good things will come to us if we just wait patiently and stay positive.

It probably feels impossible to keep a positive mindset when everything seems negative - but remember that even the toughest situations have some good aspects associated with them as well. It may be hard to see these good aspects when everything seems gloomy, but you can always find something good in any situation.

Even if you're not feeling as positive or happy as you could be, there are still plenty of ways to change things for the better. If you want to feel better about your life, then it's important that you start looking for opportunities and new ideas that can help to change your life for the better.

As long as you think positively about all the events and people in your life, it's possible for things to turn out just how you want them to. It may be difficult at first - but a positive mindset will help you get through all sorts of troubles and issues with ease.

Affirmation Meditation for

Wealth Manifestation

Wealth manifestation is among the top three wishes on most people's lists each year. The average person has a number of things they want to manifest in their lives but often don't know where to start. Affirmation meditation is a powerful process that can help you manifest your dreams and give you the confidence and conviction you need to see them through - with the added perk of increased well-being.

The Affirmation Meditation is a simple process that can be used to help manifest any of your dreams and desires. Here's the process:

1. Sit meditating with your eyes closed and focus on a particular word or phrase.

2. Expand the phrase as though it were an image in front of you.

3. Visualize what you want to manifest above, below, or on top of the phrase.

4. Repeat the phrase over and over again as if speaking it into existence.

5. Continue to repeat the phrase until you feel sure about manifestation.

6. Release the phrase or image and relax.

Here are some examples of the process in action:

1. I want to manifest a job that pays $50,000 per year and comes with health benefits.

2. (Expand image) Here is an image of me showing my boss a new business plan that will make millions.

3. (Visualize) I see a big, red building on top of my Affirmation Meditation saying: BILLIONAIRES WANTING TO BUY YOUR BUSINESS... BUY NOW!!!

4. (Repeat phrase) I see that building grow as I say: BILLIONAIRES WANTING TO BUY YOUR BUSINESS... BUY NOW!!!

5. (Relax)

6. (Release)

Affirmation meditation is a powerful way to manifest your

dreams and desires. The process can be used in the workplace, at home with your significant other, and it can also be incorporated into your daily practice. If you want to manifest your dreams, desires, and/or fears, there is no need to wait until the next "magical" month or day. Use the Affirmation Meditation now so you can manifest them today.

The saying "Money isn't everything" is a popular one in our society. This is particularly true if we examine the people who say this in a critical manner. The majority of the time, this statement is made by those who wish they had money.

The saying "Money isn't everything" is based on a faulty understanding of what money is. The origin of the statement involves a popular play in the United States called *The Racket*. In this play, every character says that money isn't everything. Unfortunately for them, money is exactly what they all wanted, and it was exactly what brought destruction upon them all.

Money IS EVERYTHING when it comes to creating heaven on earth. Money is absolutely essential if you want to live happy, free, and prosperous. It's the basic currency of earthly life. It is the means by which we can buy food, clothing, shelter, and the necessities.

The statement "Money isn't everything" is true if our minds are still limited by materialism. When we live limited lives and only think about money, it leads to problems. The real problem lies when we begin to believe that ALL things can be monetized or traded. This causes people to forget that they have a soul and they're not just things that can be bought and sold.

Affirmation meditation is powerful because it gets you to believe deeply in and remember who you really are — a spiritual being who craves love, peace, and happiness. Once you truly believe, then God (the universal source of love, peace, and happiness) will bring these things to you.

When people think in terms of money, they forget why they're on this earth and what their purpose is. They often forget that life is about more than just making money. Life is about developing relationships with others and connecting with God. Money is useful for providing the necessities of life, but it's not the only thing that matters.

An important part of this process is the term "deeply believe." The people who say "Money isn't everything" are shallow thinkers who don't deeply believe in anything. The person who truly believes in the words of money is a deep thinker. The person who has faith that "Money isn't everything" is a shallow thinker.

That's why I believe in affirmation meditation. Affirmation meditation is useful in part because it gets you to deeply believe that your dreams and desires can be manifested. When you deeply believe, the universe will deliver your wishes to you.

If you want to manifest wealth, you must deeply believe that it is possible. If we don't deeply believe in what we desire, it will not appear. Why? Because the universe only has so much energy connecting with us. By limiting our belief system (believing "You can't have this"), we block the path of manifestation.

In short, if you want money, then begin by changing your thoughts.

Sincerely believe in your true nature as a spiritual being who craves love, peace, and happiness;

Deeply believe that God is the universal source of love, peace, and happiness, and you will be able to manifest anything you desire in life. Money isn't everything; God is love, peace, and happiness.

"I know I'll manifest what I want if I deeply believe in who I am and what I want."

Every great man or woman in history has had one thing in common... These great men and women are remembered throughout history as being powerful individuals whose actions affected the lives of many people. Why is this? It's because they knew their true power - that of tapping into the universal energy reserve (aka God) to manifest whatever they wanted. They knew their own greatness, and that's why their lives have been documented for all time.

Gratitude Meditation for

Wealth Manifestation

Want to boost your wealth manifestation? Start with gratitude!

Here are ten ways gratitude meditation can help you manifest more money and material wealth:

1. Gratitude helps you release resentments, which is a great way to free up energy.

2. Gratitude helps to cleanse the aura, which makes it much easier for your manifesting efforts to work their magic. This can also give your prosperity a break by easing the stress of overworked thoughts and emotions around money or greed.

3. Gratitude helps you to release your need to control others and situations, which is an enormous pressure reliever.

4. Gratitude helps you to accept what IS. This allows a lot of magical energy and ideas that are aligned with your goals and desires to flow into your life.

5. Gratitude helps you to appreciate what people, institutions, or the universe has given you already. This frees up energy for more prosperity rather than focusing on scarcity or lack, which blocks positive money flow.

6. Gratitude helps you drop resistance and see solutions in your challenges rather than problems in your life's circumstances.

7. Gratitude helps you to see the bigger picture and trust that the seeds you plant today will grow into something beautiful tomorrow.

8. Gratitude helps you to connect with the infinite abundance of the universe and see yourself as a part of that big picture instead of separate from it. Seeing abundance as all around you is a great way to transform scarcity into prosperity!

9. Gratitude helps you feel more at peace with yourself, which is essential when manifesting prosperity because it protects you from critical inner voices or self-sabotaging behavior that can block your manifestation efforts (for example, giving away money or

opportunities for fear of looking foolish for making a mistake).

10. Gratitude helps with your manifestation process because it gives you the space to see, feel, and hear creative ideas about money or abundance that can be an invaluable resource in achieving your wealth goals.

Good luck using gratitude to manifest!

The Role of Daily Habits
in Wealth Manifestation

It's hard to escape the thought that your habits matter. Almost every recent self-help book, blog post, or educational video recommends taking on new habits in order to reach a goal. But what is it about our daily habits that make them so valuable? How do they work with manifesting wealth? And what does this have to do with the law of attraction?

In this chapter, we are going to answer these questions for you so that you can take charge of your finances and build a happy and successful life! We'll start by describing the power of habits. Then we'll dive into why new habits are so valuable for manifestation, and finally, we'll go over some simple steps you can take to start building new habits today.

Defining Habits

Let's start by defining just what a habit is exactly. What makes something a habit? When you think about it, habits are not exactly easy to define because there are so many different kinds of them, and they vary from person to person as well. However, we can try our best here and make some generalizations based on how science views habits.

A habit is a pattern of behavior that is automatic and involuntary and one that a person continues to perform on a regular basis.

A person who has many habits tends to exhibit them without even realizing it. They do things because they tend to get done. This is called habit formation. According to the scientist, habits are the result of thousands of tiny little choices we make every day, latching onto patterns that keep us going in the same direction over and over again throughout our days.

Here's how some habits form: You wake up at 7:15 AM every day . . . you get your favorite cup of coffee . . . you exercise in the morning. As you go through this process every single day, it'll eventually become a habit, and you'll no longer have to think about it. You've fully formed your habit! Habits are formed by our subconscious mind, so we have no choice or say over them. So, our subconscious creates patterns that keep us doing things automatically without even thinking about it—it forms them into habits with no resistance from us whatsoever!

This is why habits are so important to your manifestation process; if you're going through the motions of something over and over again without even thinking about it, chances are you're probably not actually seeing results. And if that's the case, you are less likely to notice that you're not seeing results when you are!

All habits tend to follow three obvious patterns:

They begin with an act of repetition. For example, you get up at 7:15 every day, so that means you'll need to walk out your front door at 7:15 every day as well.

They repeat before we can even question why . . . we've done this kind of thing before, and we'll continue doing this thing in the future. This is why habit-tracking apps can be so helpful for helping us see patterns in our behavior and how we react to different situations.

They are eventually followed by a reward. After we perform the act of repetition that formed the habit, we want something that will make us feel good in some way.

Actions Vs. Habits

Scientists in the field of psychology tell us that learning involves two types of behavior: actions and habits. The difference between these two kinds of behavior is important because they can have different impacts on our manifestation process.

When you think about it, habits are simply things that are repeated on a repetitive basis. Habits can be formed with very little conscious effort because they are automatic, unconscious, and involuntary. This is why they make the best tools to use in manifestation because they work automatically without requiring much conscious thought or effort.

Actions refer to specific behaviors or activities that we consciously choose to engage in. Unlike habits, actions are intentional and require a conscious decision or effort. Actions can be one-time occurrences or part of a larger plan or strategy. They are often driven by specific goals, motivations, or external circumstances. Unlike habits, which are typically automatic, actions require active thought and decision-making.

But habits can also have a very negative impact on our manifestation process if our habits aren't serving us in a positive way. If we are engaged in habitual behavior that we do not like or enjoy for some reason, this kind of behavior will hold us back from seeing results and enjoying the fruits of our labor. This is why it's so important to take things that we do not like or enjoy and convert them into habits rather than doing so with things we do enjoy.

In other words, forming the habit of something you don't like will cause you to resist the results it brings in your life which can actually hold you back from seeing those results. The law of attraction works because when we are resisting what it offers us, our energy is not flowing in the way it should be flowing.

For example, imagine that you like going out to dinner at nice restaurants. If you and your significant other go to a nice restaurant on a regular basis, and then you decide that you don't enjoy going out to dinner anymore, your manifestation process will hold you back from enjoying the results of your efforts because the new habit of not going out to dinner will be resisting the results that manifesting good money is supposed to bring in your life.

Now think about what it would be like if you never had the chance to enjoy eating out with friends or taking trips to different restaurants again. Imagine not visiting family or traveling somewhere just because it brings you joy. This is what it would feel like if you stopped going out to dinner with your significant other. Whenever you tried doing those things, it would most likely feel like a fight! How can we learn to work with the law of attraction when our own behavior is working against us?

Here's where the power of habits comes in. As I mentioned before, habits are unconscious, involuntary, and automatic, but they are also remarkably powerful. The law of attraction works because we can use this kind of behavior to guide our future results and the path we choose to get there.

Habits are the tool that has the power to give us what we want, so we'd better do everything in our power not to resist them!

Mindful Living Practices That Support Wealth Manifestation

Many of us spend a lot of time working and striving to acquire material things. We seem to be quite attached to the idea that these possessions will make us happy. But many psychologists, spiritual teachers, and gurus of modern science agree that this is not the truth at all!

Wealthy people have been advising for years that material possessions do not lead to happiness. Research has shown that those who are more mindful are richer in every way - their relationships, mental health, physical health, and financial well-being. And the opposite is true - the more materialistic a person is, the poorer they are, not only financially but also in all other aspects of their lives.

The reason wealth manifests in people who are more mindful is that they have a much greater appreciation of life and its subtleties. They are able to enjoy what they have rather than desire something else. It's a total shift of perspective to see life through this filter which leads to feelings of richness and gratitude. Their contentment with what they have led to an abundance of flow in every area of their life, which manifests itself as money, health, relationships, etc. What a nice place to be in!

The opposite of this is that the more materialistic a person is, the more they focus on their needs, their wants, and the things they do not have. They literally spend all their energy wishing for what they don't have, which creates an enormous amount of mental friction. This level of frustration creates inner turmoil and ultimately leads to negative effects on health and well-being. It also attracts more lack so that there is very little flow in life - just accumulation and a deepening of negativities. It is a downward spiral into the abyss. An opposite of this can be found in the mindful person.

More mindful people know how to keep their minds in balance, and they seem to have much more clarity of thought. They are able to notice the thoughts and feelings that arise, and they don't get carried away with them because they have developed a capacity for mindfulness, which means being aware of what's going on inside them and without them moment by moment. When we are caught up in our thoughts, emotions, or desires, we can't see clearly - it's like looking out at the world through a foggy window.

Mindfulness helps us to see what's really going on in our minds so that we are not at the mercy of unhealthy, destructive, or negative thoughts and emotions. It increases our happiness because we are no longer affected or weighed down by unpleasant mental states. And so we have less stress which means a healthier body!

By being more aware of the mind and its contents, you can observe how it is all interconnected. For example, if you experience depression, this might affect your motivation or ability to find work which might end up limiting your income or affecting your health, and so on - it can also work in reverse. In this way, many of our negative experiences actually create more suffering further down the line. Mindfulness helps to break this chain of negative consequences.

By being more aware, we can also see how our thoughts and feelings affect the external world around us. For example, when we think negatively, it attracts more experiences that match those thoughts. If I think "I am not good enough," I attract experiences that reinforce this belief, for example, loss of jobs, not getting an 'A' in my exams, etc. In this way, our internal states create our external circumstances and vice versa. This is the cause of so much suffering in life.

Mindfulness also brings about a sense of calm and purity. It helps us release the unnecessary layers that have become attached to our thoughts and feelings. If I am carrying around an accumulation of recent negative experiences, then when I start feeling better after practicing mindfulness, it breaks those old attachments or beliefs that are no longer useful. They are like dead, useless trees that have been rotting within me for all this time and have created all this turmoil, suffering, and negativity.

The practice of mindfulness helps to develop a new awareness system that allows us to see more clearly without getting caught up in our old patterns. This is why we get so much more from life.

Let us be careful not to misunderstand mindfulness. When we are mindful of our thoughts and feelings, we should not become attached to them. We should stay in the present moment, see things clearly and observe how they affect our experiences moment by moment. This is what brings real happiness, clarity, and wisdom into our lives!

At times, it might be helpful to have a friend with whom you can laugh or play around without letting anything get in the way of your ability to remain 'in the moment' or be truly present within yourself and in the experience of being alive! This brings a sense of calmness and joy that can only come from this clear awareness.

The awareness of your inner constitution is a kind of mirror that allows you to see yourself clearly as you really are. It is directly related to seeing the true nature of things and helps you to see how all the aspects of your life are connected.

It helps you to see what is important, what is not important, how to be happy, and the steps it will take to get there. It's a path that leads from suffering towards happiness, but instead of focusing on eliminating our problems, we look within and discover new possibilities for living a better life.

The more we practice mindfulness, the more it becomes part of our lives in every aspect - in our relationships, with ourselves, with others, with our finances, and so on. It is a way of life - or rather, a new way of living!

At times in our lives, mindfulness can become that edge that allows us to see how things really are, regardless of what we might be going through at the moment. It's an experience that is not only beneficial but necessary for the future.

Life is a series of experiences that we go through in order to get the answers to who we are and where we are going. They are like stepping stones on the journey through life - each one presents different challenges, gives us new experiences, and helps us to let some old things go. It is all very natural as this is how life works; as our inner constitution develops, it 'changes,' and we can become who we were before but more enlightened, more connected, and happier. It's a process of growth and progress!

When we practice mindfulness, it becomes easier for us to experience the changes, both internally and externally, that bring about greater happiness, joy, and contentment. In addition, it helps bring about greater stability in our lives.

The practice of mindfulness is effective in helping us to see things clearly and as they really are. It helps us to minimize our suffering and increase our happiness. It brings about a sense of compassion for ourselves and others, which allows us to step back from our negative experiences so that we don't take them too seriously or give in to the negative thoughts and emotions that follow.

We can then begin to notice the way we tend to spend all of

our time trying to satisfy a whole list of desires - materialistic, emotional, and mental ones - instead of living to find out what it means to be happy.

Achieving Abundance and Financial Prosperity Through Meditation and Positive Mindset

Our society is so focused on the material side of life — finding a good job, earning more money, buying bigger houses and newer cars--that we lose sight of what really matters. This is not to say that these things are unimportant, but rather that they are only one piece of our whole life experience.

In this chapter, we'll explore how meditation and a positive mindset can enable you to achieve abundance and financial prosperity in whatever form you desire or need it. We'll share some tips for high-achieving people who want to do more with their lives, as well as for people who live near or below the poverty line and want to find new opportunities for betterment.

If you're happy and secure with your way of life and don't feel the need to change anything, it's okay. But if you feel that there is more out there for you to do, we want to share some of our personal experiences as well as research on meditation and positive mindset.

This chapter will give you a few ideas of how meditation and a positive mindset can benefit your life in multiple ways.

Here are some examples of how money and material possessions can be used as tools to achieve your goals or dreams.

Money itself comes from a place of abundance, as does our time. As human beings, we have only so many hours in each day. If we want to accomplish more with our time, it's important to use that time wisely and not just waste it away buying things that are no longer useful to us or don't bring any benefit to our life. Remembering this and building positive habits of saving something for the future can expand your life beyond what you could ever imagine.

Meditation can take a lot of your stress away, making you more confident, relaxed, and happier. It can also help you reduce your tendency to worry and help you make better decisions in life. This, in turn, helps you build your confidence and make better choices in life. When you are more confident and happy with what happens to you in life, it makes it easier for you to use these tools to achieve more goals.

A positive mindset has been shown to be an important factor in the financial success of people who have achieved extreme wealth through entrepreneurship or investing strategies compared with those who did not feel that their success was a result of their own efforts. A few of the study's findings were that those with a positive mindset demonstrated significantly greater persistence, optimism, and motivation than their more pessimistic counterparts.

It's very important to be confident in what you are doing and have a positive attitude because our actions influence our results. A positive mindset is not some magical power that we all possess; rather, it is something that we can cultivate by learning from our experiences.

The world will reward those who are clear about their goals, as well as those who are able to recognize opportunities for success and capitalize on them. When you start on the road to achieving abundance and financial prosperity, it's good to have a clear picture of what you want to achieve.

To do this, it's good to prepare your mind for abundance in all areas of life: physical health, mental health (competence and confidence), happiness, wealth, and relationships. You have probably already noticed that the way we feel about something colors the way in which we experience it. If you visualize abundance before starting your day, this will help you achieve better results. It's important to use meditation when doing this because it helps relax both your mind and body, so they are more receptive to these positive thoughts.

We can do this through meditation by envisioning all the things we want to achieve, connecting with our unique internal power, and then breathing deeply. This is a great way to get started on the road to abundance and financial prosperity.

If you want more financial abundance in your life, here are some ways it can help you achieve that:

For example, if you want to be more creative and inventive, it will require you to take time out of your day to think about innovative ideas and then experiment with them. This, in turn, requires a lot of time and energy.

The ancient Vedic texts have long espoused that meditation has the power to heal, improve memory, and create wealth.

In recent years scientists have been lending support to this idea by linking meditation and a positive mindset with a variety of health benefits. Although it is likely true that there are many paths to achieving success in life, I do believe that, more often than not, we are too focused on the physical needs of life getting in the way of our spiritual pursuits. Some of us make the choice to ignore the high priority we should be giving to our spiritual needs. But you don't have to look too hard in this world to see that people are more unhappy, unhealthy, and broke than ever before. This imbalance is leading people down a path toward chronic disease, unhappiness, and overall emptiness.

So I believe it's worth taking a look at how you can use meditation as a foundation for your everyday life activities. To help illustrate this point, I would like to share a story about my master Baba Ram Dass and two of the most influential men of the 20th Century. I hope this inspires you to make the most of your own meditation practice so that you can reach your full potential in life.

An anonymous shares his story on positive mindset:

In the early 70s, Baba Ram Dass was living as a monk at a

house in Huntington, New York, that was frequented by two of the most important people of the 20th century, Richard Alpert and Timothy Leary. As legend has it, their time at this house was when they came up with the idea for their new movement called "Psychedelic," which promoted the use of psychedelic drugs to help achieve higher states of consciousness. Alpert stated that he first tried LSD in the basement of this house with Ram Dass, and at the time, it was called "Owsley acid."

It was on Christmas Eve of 1968 that I saw Baba for the first time on a snowy road leading to his house. He was coming to visit my friend, who had been living at the Huntington house for two years by then. By pure chance, I had just arrived from India, and my friend asked Baba if I could please stay with him rather than go back overseas. So Baba took me under his wing, which included many hours a day of meditation, intense discussions about life, as well as lots of sharing in good food and laughter. It was within this environment that I began to learn about the spiritual practice of meditation, and in many ways, it changed my life.

Over a lifetime of living with Baba as my friend and teacher, I was able to learn a lot about meditation, but his primary message was that we should all meditate to have greater happiness in our lives. Baba taught me nada yoga, which is a yoga of sound or mantra meditation. On many occasions, he would say this to people who came to visit him: "Please do not come here unless you are ready to help people. What I really need here in America is some real meditators. Most people who come here really don't know what to do with themselves, even though they regularly sit for hours a day in meditation. Most of them don't make it a priority in their life. If this is the case, then I need you here. "

Baba explained that he had to give up many things in order to live as a monk and meditate 20 hours a day. At times he would even fast as he meditated. It was one of his strongest reasons for doing so, which was the ability to stay present and alert through meditation which enabled him to "see what is going on behind the screen," which would then allow him not just to understand these things better but also predict their future course of action. Baba also explained that he didn't want to miss out on anything in life, which was why he was willing to make this major sacrifice for his spiritual growth.

Baba said that people were coming from all over the world to learn from him, and it was because they wanted to "learn how to see what is going on behind the screen," as he put it.

These days we may have heard this described as "seeing through the illusion"; however, Baba would use other words such as "get back behind the screen." He would tell me that meditation gets you back behind the screen where you can see what is going on and even hear what others are saying. Baba said that the more you practice, the more you can see what is going on behind the screen.

As I learned later from my studies of the ancient Vedic texts and other wisdom traditions, this is exactly how you learn to be a seer or Rishi. You learn to see what's going on behind the screen. You get back behind it or behind the illusion. The problem is most people don't practice enough meditation to get back there. And once there, they don't know what they are supposed to do when they get there. This is why so few people actually become spiritually enlightened, because of this lack of understanding of the process.

When I met Baba, he was already a well-known spiritual teacher, yet what I learned from him over the years was more than anything else about meditation and its transform-ative power. As I gradually learned to meditate for one hour every day, I also noticed that my life started to change in many ways. Although it's too vast a subject to discuss here, we all have areas where we could use some improvement, whether it's stress or lack of energy or depression, or feeling stuck in life's challenges. Most of us spend lots of time trying to improve these things by taking pills, seeing doctors, or trying various treatments and therapies. But the truth is most of them don't really work.

During the last 40 years, I have seen countless people who have tried various medical and other treatments, either because they were told they needed to or, in many cases, they just wanted to feel better. As a result of my own experiences trying all of these different treatments, I can say with certainty that our modern biomedical approach is flawed and that there is a whole new way we can improve our health and well-being through meditation. There are hundreds of studies already done on meditation research, and any one of them would give you a good idea about how beneficial it can be for your health.

On this subject, Baba would often say: "The problem is that our approach to life is not working. It's bound to fail, and when people get sick, it doesn't help them out of their suffering. All they do is take a pill that stops their body from feeling bad, but the real suffering still remains inside." The point he made was that taking pills can mask symptoms, but they don't deal with the root cause of many chronic diseases and often merely add years to one's health rather than quality to one's life.

Baba would also say, "If you want to live a happy and healthy life, you need a root cause that can be dealt with. What we do here is just slather medication on top of the problem, which may dull the symptoms, but it doesn't really solve anything. We don't have enough people practicing meditation so that they know how to get back behind the screen." I remember hearing Baba say this often, so it has stuck in my mind, and I will quote him directly here: "I don't think most people know how to do this. It's not like we can teach them. They must learn by themselves. If you want to become enlightened, then you need your own personal teacher."

How to Manifest Self-Love

You've probably come across the term "manifesting" on social media or in the popular new-age self-help section of bookstores. As someone who avidly consumes such material, I understand the fascination. However, if you're unfamiliar with the concept, don't worry, my friend.

How to Cultivate Self-Love Through Manifestation

Enhance self-awareness of your current self-perception.

Before embarking on the journey of manifesting a different reality, it's crucial to comprehend your starting point. Ask yourself: How do you truly feel about being yourself? Which aspects of yourself do you find most challenging to accept? And when are you most critical of yourself? Gaining clarity on your level of self-acceptance (remember, this is just the starting point) will provide direction for your progress.

Envision the desired state of being.

How would you like to feel about yourself? What judgments and criticisms would you like to let go of? When you gaze at your reflection, how do you want to feel about inhabiting your own skin? Creating a vivid mental image of your desired state is a vital step in manifesting self-love. Having a clear vision of your destination enables you to immerse yourself in this new way of being, to glimpse the possibilities and potentials of this reality. This self-image, depicting acceptance, honor, and love for yourself, serves as the focal point of your efforts. You can conjure this image whenever needed to remind yourself of how your life could feel. If you can visualize it, you can work towards it.

Express your desires.

Traditional manifesting involves the important step of expressing your wishes, intentions, or requests to the universe. Once you've put it out there, your role is to open yourself up to the possibility of it coming true (in other words, don't hinder the positive things that come your way by self-sabotaging or denying affirming messages). You don't necessarily have to address your request or intention to the "universe" per se – tailor it to suit your preferences! Remember, you're in charge. You can connect with a force that resonates with you, be it through prayer to God, seeking assistance from the "Source," or establishing a connection with your own spiritual essence through meditation. Perhaps you can simply verbalize your intention or wish aloud without concerning yourself with who or what may be listening. The key is to be specific about what you desire and put it out into the world. You can journal about your desired outcome, write notes to yourself in lipstick on your bathroom mirror, or place reminders on your phone or in unexpected places. Daily reminders of your aspirations are essential. If you want to cultivate greater love and acceptance for yourself, consciously bring these thoughts into your awareness each day.

Take deliberate action.

Manifesting involves trusting that your message has been heard by the universe and that your dreams are on their way to you. However, it's not as simple as just waiting passively. While keeping the image of your preferred self in mind every day, you also need to take intentional action to move in the right direction. For instance, if you want to be kinder to yourself but constantly cringe at your wrinkles when looking in the mirror, you're not taking responsibility for change. Identify the unloving ways you think about or treat yourself (as mentioned in step 1) and outline clear steps to overcome these negative patterns. For example, suppose you often lie in bed at night, reviewing all the ways you feel like a "failed" mom that day, drowning in guilt and regret over conversations with your children. In that case, you can plan for this recurring pattern. When these thoughts arise (remember, they are just thoughts and not necessarily the truth), you have a choice. Will you continue down the path of self-criticism, or will you change it? What if you said to yourself: "Those were challenging moments today. I feel remorseful about how I spoke, but I also understand why I was frustrated. I have a lot on my plate, and I'm doing my best. My kids know they are loved." This simple exercise in self-compassion, acknowledging and understanding your behavior, can significantly alleviate self-judgment.

Embrace receptivity.

According to the original concept of manifesting, once you express your desires, be prepared because they are on their way to you! To welcome positive outcomes, we need to be open and receptive. If we go through life with a defensive mindset, we hinder the arrival of good things, such as meaningful interactions, supportive people, and positive emotions. In other words, be willing to see your vision of self-love materialize. Allow yourself to entertain the possibility that it could become a reality. This can be challenging, especially if you have spent many years struggling with self-loathing or battling a harsh inner critic. Instead of resigning yourself to perpetual self-judgment, perfectionism, or judgmental thoughts, reframe these aspects. Acknowledge that while you may have exhibited these traits in the past, you are now ready to experience a different way of being. Even if you have always been critical when you see your reflection, embrace the excitement of a new experience. Staying open to new thoughts and perspectives about yourself is essential. When positive experiences do occur (for example, feeling proud of your parenting at the end of the day), embrace them wholeheartedly. Notice the difference, experience acceptance, and don't dismiss these moments.

As you work on cultivating self-love, I encourage you to actively search for evidence of your progress. Ask yourself: What small changes have I made? Does my inner voice sound more nurturing? Have I become more self-compassionate and forgiving? Is there anything I feel proud of lately? Shedding light on these new experiences of self-love, regardless of their magnitude, is crucial in this process. You need to observe the impact of your intentions.

Cultivate self-kindness and compassion.

Remember, it has taken your entire life to shape the person you are at this moment. Automatic thoughts, particularly critical ones, may have been reinforced over a long period. Therefore, don't be surprised if they persist for a while. Most importantly, recognize that thoughts are just thoughts. They are not always reflective of the truth and are often deeply ingrained habits. If you find yourself slipping back into self-criticism and loathing (which may happen from time to time), challenge yourself to see it as an old pattern and return to a place of self-compassion. Thoughts are products of routines and patterns. If you allow yourself to dwell in negativity, you'll remain trapped. However, by intentionally cultivating self-kindness and love through the power of manifestation, you'll attract more of these positive qualities into your life.

10 Self-Care Quotes and Affirmations:

Manifesting Self Love

Do you sometimes feel depleted? If so, why not nourish your whole self by reading and manifesting these powerful self-care quotes and affirmations? In this busy world, it is way too easy to forget to care for ourselves. We all do it! And yet;

- Physical exhaustion makes us sad.
- Emotional turmoil drains energy weakening the body and our spirit.
- Feeling lost brings our spirits down and makes us doubt ourselves.
- Too much to do all the time makes us scatty, angry, and easily overwhelmed.

Self-care is a practical means of looking after our well-being.

Our 1:1 client work and group retreats distinctly show that

caring for our body, heart, mind, and spirit is a concrete way to nurture balance, peace and serenity, joy, and most importantly, self-love. Whether you're a student, artist, professional, an academic or researcher, or stay-at-home parent – today's world is a busy world. Practical and concrete reminders can help. This is why we've put together these ten self-care affirmations for you from a range of people with wisdom we admire and follow.

10 Self-Care Affirmations

Affirmations are short wisdom statements that reaffirm deep truths. They can help us do well and be well.

Use them to:

- Reframe how you see things.
- Remind you about what matters.
- Manage your mood.
- Improve how you see and treat yourself.
- Keep in good form.
- Improve your productivity.
- Begin to recognize habits you need to shed.
- Put an end to drifting or languishing.

- Motivate positive action.
- Stimulate a useful re-think.
- Reconnect with compassion.
- Support inner balance and harmony.
- Create new goals.
- Highlight what's true.
- Learn about yourself.

Here are ten powerful self-care affirmations that can help you to manifest self-love:

1. I am deserving of love and care, and I prioritize my well-being.
2. I am worthy of taking time for myself and nurturing my mind, body, and spirit.
3. I release any guilt or shame associated with self-care and embrace it as a vital part of my life.
4. I am in control of my own happiness, and I choose to prioritize my mental and emotional health.
5. I acknowledge my strengths and achievements and celebrate myself regularly.
6. I let go of the need to please everyone and set healthy boundaries that honor my needs and limits.
7. I am capable of handling challenges, and I trust myself to find solutions and grow from adversity.

8. I am allowed to rest and recharge without feeling guilty, as it is essential for my overall well-being.

9. I am worthy of pursuing my passions and investing time in activities that bring me joy and fulfillment.

10. I choose to surround myself with positive and supportive people who uplift and encourage me in my self-care journey.

If a particular picture or affirmation spoke deeply to you, consider sharing this article with someone who would benefit as well. Let's spread kindness towards ourselves and others.

10 Self-Care Quotes

Self-care quotes for self-love encapsulate the essence of taking care of oneself and nurturing a healthy relationship with oneself. These quotes emphasize the importance of prioritizing personal well-being, both physically and emotionally. They serve as reminders to practice self-compassion, self-acceptance, and self-respect. Here are ten powerful self-care quotes that promote self-love:

1. "Self-care is not selfish; it is essential for your well-being."

2. "You are deserving of your own love and care, just as much as anyone else."

3. "Self-love is the foundation for a happy and fulfilling life."

4. "Nourish your mind, body, and soul because you deserve to thrive."

5. "Self-care is not a luxury; it's a necessity for self-growth and resilience."

6. "Your relationship with yourself sets the tone for every other relationship in your life."

7. "Caring for yourself is an act of self-respect and self-empowerment."

8. "You owe yourself the same love, kindness, and compassion that you so freely give to others."

9. "Prioritizing self-care is a powerful declaration of your worthiness."

10. "Remember, self-love is not about being perfect; it's about embracing your imperfections and loving yourself unconditionally."

How to Manifest Anything You Desire

Yes, that even includes love...and money.

Assisting you in achieving the life you desire is a significant objective of Oprah Daily and Oprah herself. Through our exclusive "Life You Want" classes and events, our community of readers learns the art of intentional living, from creating vision boards to embracing forgiveness. Another powerful approach to living your best life is through manifestation.

Manifestation, also known as the laws of attraction, may already be familiar to you. It gained considerable attention through the bestselling book "The Secret" in 2006, authored by Rhonda Byrne, selling over 30 million copies. Esteemed thought leaders like Deepak Chopra, Eckhart Tolle, Gabrielle Bernstein, Iyanla Vanzant, and Oprah herself have spoken about it, all in agreement that manifestation is a tangible reality.

However, it's crucial to understand that manifestation is not an instant process. While it involves turning your dreams into reality, it demands proactive steps toward your desires. While it may take time, the profound impact it can have on your life makes it a worthwhile investment.

In our "The Life You Want" planner, an effective tool for goal-setting and intentional living, Oprah emphasizes the importance of having a vision. She writes, "Having a vision creates a path for the future. It helps you to focus and allows for clarity moving forward." In a conversation with LinkedIn CEO Jeff Weiner in 2015, Oprah further explored the power of manifestation, stating, "You control a lot by your thoughts. When I started to figure that out, I was like, What else can I do? What else can I manifest? Because I have seen it work. I have seen it happen over and over again."

If you're ready to give manifestation a try, here are the expert-recommended steps to manifest anything you desire, including love and money.

But first, let's clarify what manifestation entails exactly.

Manifestation is the process of attracting and believing in something tangible to enter your life. It goes beyond sheer willpower and positive thinking. As Angelina Lombardo, author of "Spiritual Entrepreneur," explains, manifestation involves turning your desired feelings and experiences into reality through your thoughts, actions, beliefs, and emotions.

To initiate manifestation, it is crucial to have clear goals.

While each person may approach manifestation differently, Lombardo suggests that most adhere to the same fundamental principles. First and foremost, you must have a precise understanding of what you want. Lombardo asserts, "You are the only one who dreams your dreams, so whether it's a new partner and a healthy relationship or a better job, know it and own it." Regardless of your desires, specificity is key. Instead of merely stating, "I want to meet my soulmate," develop a vivid image of their qualities, characteristics, and values.

Once you have set your intention, it is essential to articulate it and write it down.

After identifying your hopes, dreams, and goals with clarity, you must articulate your desires to the universe. This can be done through various methods such as prayer, meditation, visualization, speaking your intentions aloud, creating a vision board, or even using a "future box" filled with pictures representing your desired manifestations. Writing down your intentions is also highly effective. The popular 369 methods, where you write your desires three times in the morning, six times in the afternoon, and nine times at night for 33 or 45 days, has gained traction on platforms like Tik-Tok. Alternatively, a simple letter to the universe can also suffice.

Simultaneously, take actionable steps toward your goals.

According to Gabrielle Bernstein, author of "Super Attractor" and "The Universe Has Your Back," manifestation is a collaborative process between you and the universe. Merely knowing what you want is only half the battle; results won't manifest without action. Allocate time to contemplate the steps you can personally take to achieve your goals and incorporate them into your routine. For instance, if you aim to make a significant career change, start networking with professionals in your desired field and practice for job interviews.

Lombardo adds, "Another way to be 'in action' when manifesting is to ask yourself, 'What would my future self be thinking?'" By reframing your mindset, you increase your chances of success. Becoming the person who already possesses, does, and feels your desired goals and dreams paves the way for their realization.

Furthermore, practice mindfulness and gratitude for what you receive.

While you may not receive everything you envision in the exact order or timeframe you desire, it is crucial to acknowledge and appreciate what you do receive, regardless of its size. Gratitude plays a key role, and maintaining a gratitude journal can be immensely helpful. Dedicate five to ten minutes before bed to write down things you are grateful for and any occurrences that bring you closer to your manifestations. Perhaps you save money for retirement, and you receive a call from your cable provider offering a way to reduce your monthly bill, or you stumble upon an inspiring podcast that sparks an idea for a lucrative side hustle.

Release resistance and limiting beliefs.

In addition to transforming your mindset and behaviors, it is essential to let go of any obstacles or limiting beliefs that obstruct your vision. Fear and negative self-talk can cloud your path. Oprah highlighted this during an episode of "Oprah's Lifeclass," saying, "Telling yourself you're not good enough, you're not worthy enough, you're not smart enough, you're not enough—it's a tape that's playing for a lot of people. If you're not conscious of that, then you end up acting out of that belief system and not what you know to be the truest or want to be the truest for yourself. You don't become what you want because so much of wanting is about living in the space of what you don't have."

To overcome these limiting beliefs, start by identifying them. Ask yourself what beliefs you hold about yourself that might hinder your progress. Write down your answers and then replace the limiting beliefs with empowering affirmations. For example, if you believe you are incomplete without a partner, affirm that you are whole as you are. If you think you're not good enough, affirm that you are wonderful as you are today. Additionally, whenever you find yourself questioning your worth, take a moment to acknowledge the reasons why you deserve the manifestations you desire.

Lastly, pay attention to and cultivate positive energy.

Oprah emphasizes the significance of energy, stating, "The energy we put out in the world is the energy we get back." According to her Super Soul Conversation with Michael Bernard Beckwith, if you consistently emit negative energy through your thoughts or emotions, you will attract the same negativity back into your life. Conversely, shifting your energy and raising your vibrations will attract positivity and accelerate the realization of your goals.

Fortunately, elevating your energy is simple. Engage in activities that bring you joy and happiness, whether it's performing acts of kindness, starting your day with meditation or yoga, spending time in nature, or indulging in self-care.

By following these steps, you can master the art of manifestation and create the life you desire, including love and financial abundance.

Conclusion

You can also focus on cultivating your desired feelings, as advised by Oprah. She suggests, "If you wish to experience more love in your life, set your intention to be more loving. If kindness is what you seek, direct your energy towards empathy and compassion."

However, it's important to remain adaptable and trust the process. The manifestation journey is fluid, and the specific steps you take are not as crucial as your belief in the process. As Angelina Lombardo states, "Have faith in your actions, visions, and clarity, as well as the higher powers." Faith is a potent motivator and guiding force.

Indeed, you have the ability to manifest love. The beauty of manifestation lies in its limitless possibilities. The law of attraction knows no boundaries. Lombardo explains, "Once you begin honing your manifestation process, there are no limits to what or how frequently or abundantly you can manifest." This includes fostering new friendships and romantic relationships. However, it is essential to manifest individuals who support your goals. Lombardo advises, "You should only attract people who are drawn to the person you are becoming. While this might mean excluding some exciting prospects, you'll be happier with someone who aligns with the version of you that's making significant progress." Remember, manifesting love, like anything else, requires genuine effort.

The same principles apply to manifesting money. The process for manifesting financial abundance follows the steps mentioned earlier. Marla McKenna, the author of Manifesting Your Dreams, emphasizes that gratitude (along with effort) is the foundation of financial manifestation. "To manifest money, it's crucial to acknowledge the abundance you already possess and express gratitude for it," explains Bill McKenna. "Even when facing financial challenges, elevate your vibrational frequency and eliminate any limiting beliefs by welcoming the money and prosperity that is on its way. In essence, focus on what you have rather than what you lack." McKenna also suggests utilizing visual tools to stay motivated and focused, such as purchasing a larger purse, visualizing swimming in a pool of cash, creating a money tree with fake money until you can replace it with real money, or writing a substantial check to yourself, knowing that one day you will cash it.

What's the most efficient way to manifest something you desire? According to McKenna, if you can visualize and feel it, you can achieve it. "The simplest way to manifest anything is to be clear about your desires. Avoid sending mixed signals to the universe and take action. It is essential to actively work towards your goals." Additionally, it's crucial to remain open and receptive. Ask the universe for what you want and remain attentive to signs of progress or success. McKenna reminds us, "The only thing standing in the way of manifesting your dreams is you. What you can envision in your mind, you can hold in your hands. So, get to work! You have manifesting to do!"

References

https://jackcanfield.com/blog/manifesting-money/

https://www.everlur.com/blogs/everlur/manifestation-myths

https://www.mindbodygreen.com/articles/the-12-universal-laws-and-how-to-practice-them

https://sarahscoop.com/25-ways-on-how-to-manifest-positive-energy-in-your-life/

https://lemetropolelille.com/is-manifesting-a-sin/

https://amen.io/blog/is-manifesting-a-sin

https://timesofindia.indiatimes.com/readersblog/justthoughtss/manifestation-is-not-magic-47319/

https://www.mindbodygreen.com/articles/the-12-universal-laws-and-how-to-practice-them

https://kateborsato.com/blog-articles/how-to-manifest-self-love/

https://www.oprahdaily.com/life/a30244004/how-to-manifest-anything/

Made in United States
North Haven, CT
25 July 2024

55444404R00095